Piano Chords

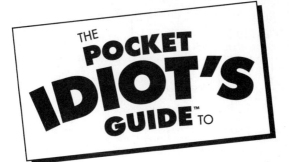

Piano Chords

by Karen Berger

ALPHA

A member of Penguin Group (USA) Inc.

ALPHA BOOKS

Published by the Penguin Group

Penguin Group (USA) Inc., 375 Hudson Street, New York, New York 10014, U.S.A.

Penguin Group (Canada), 10 Alcorn Avenue, Toronto, Ontario, Canada M4V 3B2 (a division of Pearson Penguin Canada Inc.)

Penguin Books Ltd, 80 Strand, London WC2R 0RL, England

Penguin Ireland, 25 St Stephen's Green, Dublin 2, Ireland (a division of Penguin Books Ltd)

Penguin Group (Australia), 250 Camberwell Road, Camberwell, Victoria 3124, Australia (a division of Pearson Australia Group Pty Ltd)

Penguin Books India Pvt Ltd, 11 Community Centre, Panchsheel Park, New Delhi—110 017, India

Penguin Group (NZ), cnr Airborne and Rosedale Roads, Albany, Auckland 1310, New Zealand (a division of Pearson New Zealand Ltd)

Penguin Books (South Africa) (Pty) Ltd, 24 Sturdee Avenue, Rosebank, Johannesburg 2196, South Africa

Penguin Books Ltd, Registered Offices: 80 Strand, London WC2R 0RL, England

Copyright © 2005 by Karen Berger

International Standard Book Number: 1-59257-459-9
Library of Congress Catalog Card Number: 2005908682

08 07 06 05   8 7 6 5 4 3 2 1

Interpretation of the printing code: The rightmost number of the first series of numbers is the year of the book's printing; the rightmost number of the second series of numbers is the number of the book's printing. For example, a printing code of 05-1 shows that the first printing occurred in 2005.

Printed in the United States of America

Note: This publication contains the opinions and ideas of its author. It is intended to provide helpful and informative material on the subject matter cov-ered. It is sold with the understanding that the author and publisher are not engaged in rendering professional services in the book. If the reader requires personal assistance or advice, a competent professional should be consulted.

The author and publisher specifically disclaim any responsibility for any liabil-ity, loss, or risk, personal or otherwise, which is incurred as a consequence, directly or indirectly, of the use and application of any of the contents of this book.

Most Alpha books are available at special quantity discounts for bulk purchases for sales promotions, premiums, fund-raising, or educational use. Special books, or book excerpts, can also be created to fit specific needs.

For details, write: Special Markets, Alpha Books, 375 Hudson Street, New York, NY 10014.

This book is gratefully dedicated to my parents, Zdenek and Lorna Berger, for many years of piano lessons.

Contents

Appendixes

Introduction

When I was a kid, complete strangers would buttonhole me at piano recitals: "Don't quit!" they'd urge, then launch into some rambling story about how they gave up piano and now it was too late to learn. Or they were afraid it would be too difficult.

Too late to learn? Nonsense! And it's not as hard as you think—no matter how successful (or not) your early attempts at piano may have been.

Perhaps you had lessons in the distant past and wish you had stuck with it. Perhaps you've never played, but have always been drawn to the piano. Or perhaps you're starting lessons now and you're wondering whether it's always going to be this confusing.

There's no question that playing the piano can be complicated: the instrument wouldn't have fascinated composers and players for 300-plus years if there wasn't a lot you can do with it.

But I'm going to tell you a secret: much of what those composers have been doing for all those years is based on a few fairly simple concepts. When you know how to recognize the patterns, you'll see (and hear) the same sounds popping up over and over again—whether you're listening to Bach or the blues. And that makes learning to play the piano a most manageable task.

So why does it seem so hard?

If you have any experience with classical music lessons, you probably remember spending lots of time trying to make your fingers obey your brain. Then there were those hieroglyphics: all those dots and lines you had to read. And at the same time, your teacher was beating time in the background.

The classical style of learning teaches you how to play from sheet music, which means that you learn how to follow a composer's detailed set of instructions. Sheet music is used for playing classical music, and it's also available for popular songs. But if your goal is to play popular songs, this traditional approach is like shooting a mosquito with a cannon: it's overkill. You don't need to spend years learning advanced technique to play songs on the piano.

In fact, many jazz pianists and keyboard players in rock groups don't have traditional training, and some gigging pianists aren't even that good at reading music. More often, they use the chord approach, in which the sheet music consists only of the basic melody and a set of instructions telling you which chords to play. The chord approach is so streamlined and effective for jazz and pop that it's used even by musicians who do have traditional training.

The beauty of the chord approach is that after you learn the rules, you can make up your own accompaniments. This method lets even a rank beginner play a complete song—yet gives you all the information you need to build truly original, complex arrangements of your favorite tunes.

Chord Approach

So what is this chord approach?

Chords are groups of three or four (or more) notes that are played together. In a basic arrangement of a song, your right hand plays the melody while your left hand plays chords—groups of notes that sound good with that melody. As you become more skilled, you can add little flourishes and variations, make big noisy chords or soft supple ones, and create a version of a song that is uniquely your own. The player, in effect, becomes a co-creator along with the composer.

The chord approach is completely different from traditional piano lessons. The two approaches complement each other, but they don't lead to the same place. Believe it or not, a well-trained traditional player may be able to play a Chopin étude with flying fingers—but ask him to come up with a spur-of-the-moment finger-snapping version of "Happy Birthday," and you might be out of luck. On the other hand, while learning chords will give you the tools to play thousands of songs, it won't give you the skills to play a Rachmaninoff concerto at Carnegie Hall. Then again, if you were thinking of being a concert pianist, you wouldn't be reading this book.

Who This Book Is For

Let's be clear: this book is not for aspiring concert pianists. It will not teach you how to play Mozart or Chopin, and it may not even get you an invitation to jam at your local jazz club.

What this book will do is give you the tools and information you need to play songs—songs you like, songs your kids know, songs your family used to sing at Christmas. It doesn't take years of technique drills to be able to play chords and melodies. What it does take is the curiosity to think about how music is put together, and a willingness to make some really noisy mistakes.

It also takes commitment—although of the most enjoyable sort. I'm not going to dazzle you with false promises: playing the piano well takes practice and a willingness to exercise your brain as much as your fingers. At first, the learning curve may seem steep. After spending hundreds of hours teaching adults, I've come to the conclusion that one of the main differences between beginning and advanced pianists is that advanced pianists accept a certain amount of frustration as a fact of life. We don't expect to play a tune perfectly the first time, and we don't expect immediate results. What we know—and perhaps the most important secret I can share with you—is that if we show up at the keyboard, we will learn to play.

"Showing up" means experimenting, thinking, practicing, and playing—in the true, childlike sense of the word. Learning the piano is not a controllable process. Your progress will in part depend on your prior musical experience and your unique set of talents. (Good ear? Quick at reading? Agile fingers? Solid sense of rhythm?) But most of all, it depends on your desire. This book gives you the tools. But a toolbox doesn't build a house: A person using those tools builds a house. And it's the same with playing the piano.

Your job is to have fun.

Extras

The sidebars in this book are designed to add extra bits of information that will clear up possible confusion, give you practice hints to master a technique, and explain some concepts in more detail.

 Universal Language _____

Music is often called "the universal language"—but this is a language with its own lingo. If you can't tell your bass clef from your treble clef, or think that andante is how you like your pasta, look to these boxes for a translation.

 Practice Makes Perfect _____

You already know the tired old joke about the way to Carnegie Hall, right? Practice. These short exercises and practical tips will get your fingers moving and help you feel comfortable at the keyboard.

Music to Your Ears _____

Music is filled with fun little factoids, some of them useful for playing and others useful for dazzling your dinner companions. Here we give you information that will intrigue and inspire you.

Sour Notes _____

Mistakes are an inevitable part of the process of learning an instrument—and sometimes the source for real inspiration. But there's no need to overdo the "trial" part of "trial and error." This section offers tips for avoiding common mistakes and pitfalls.

Acknowledgments

I'd like to thank my agent, Marilyn Allen, for making this project possible. Thanks to Mike Sanders for speeding it along, and editors Keith Cline, Nancy Lewis, and Billy Fields for pulling it together. I'd also like to thank Jane Blackstone for sharing her knowledge about piano chords and jazz theory with me, and David Hodge for his insights into teaching music by writing about it.

Trademarks

All terms mentioned in this book that are known to be or are suspected of being trademarks or service marks have been appropriately capitalized. Alpha Books and Penguin Group (USA) Inc. cannot attest to the accuracy of this information. Use of a term in this book should not be regarded as affecting the validity of any trademark or service mark.

Chapter 1

Keyboard Geography

In This Chapter

- Learning how notes are organized and named
- Measuring distances between notes
- Understanding basic finger placement
- Starting-out exercises

Like any good trip, our musical journey begins with a map—in this case, a map of the piano. It doesn't matter whether you are playing on a concert grand, a small upright, or an electronic keyboard. All piano keyboards look pretty much the same. Some electronic keyboards have fewer keys than full-size pianos, but the keys they do have are still organized the same way.

This chapter covers where the notes are, how they are named, and how you measure the distance between notes. The reason we're worried about measuring distances isn't because we've taken the map metaphor too far—it's because that's how you'll learn to build different kinds of chords.

The basics of knowing where you are on the piano isn't rocket science: if you know the first seven letters of the alphabet, you've got the hard part licked. But somehow, you need to get this knowledge from your brain into your fingers. The best way to do this is to spend time at the keyboard. The practice suggestions in this chapter will help you get your fingers moving. You can also invent your own exercises. But whatever you do, don't read this book in one uninterrupted sitting! Get up and go to the piano! See what the notes and chords actually sound like.

High Notes, Low Notes, Black Notes, White Notes

Let's start by getting our bearings (see Figure 1.1). You'll often hear musicians talk about high notes and low notes, leaving you to wonder exactly which way is up on a horizontal instrument like the piano.

Simple: The lowest note on a keyboard is on the farthest left. You move "up" the keyboard by moving to the right.

    lower notes   mid-range notes   higher notes

Figure 1.1 *Low notes are to the left, high notes to the right.*

Try it: play a few notes on the left side of the piano. These are the notes the basses would bellow, or the tuba would toot. As you move up the keyboard (to the right), you get into mid-range territory—think of the mellow tones of violas or clarinets. And then, on the far-right side, you've got your nosebleed territory where the sopranos, violins, and piccolos hang out.

You'll also notice that the piano is divided into black keys and white keys. A lot of beginning players assume the black keys mean trouble: they think that black keys are somehow harder or more complicated than the white keys. Not so! The black keys work exactly the same way as the white keys: The low ones are at the left, and the high ones are at the right.

If you want to play all the keys on the piano in order, you start at the lowest white key, then play the very next key to its right, regardless of whether it is white or black (see Figure 1.2). Then you play the next key (again, regardless of whether it is black or white). And so on.

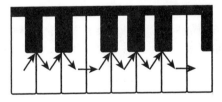

Figure 1.2 *Going up the keyboard, one note at a time.*

Listen carefully as you play the black keys and white keys in order. Close your eyes. There's no special "black key sound," is there? The sound of a black key is halfway between the sounds of the white keys on either side of it.

The Musical Alphabet: Easier Than ABC

The musical alphabet consists of just seven notes, named after the first seven letters of the alphabet: A, B, C, D, E, F, and G. These names are given to the white notes. (We'll get to the black notes in just a minute.) After you get to G, the note names start all over again, and they repeat all the way up the keyboard.

But which note is which?

Notice that the black keys are organized into groups of two and three. These groupings are repeated up and down the piano. Having these in repeated, regular patterns makes it easy to find any note anywhere.

Here's how: find a group of two black keys. Now play the white key that is to the immediate left of these two black keys. This note is a C (see Figure 1.3). Any white key anywhere on the piano that is just to the left of a group of two black keys is a C.

Figure 1.3 *A C is always just to the left of a group of two black keys.*

Play two or three Cs. Middle C is the C closest to the middle of the keyboard—on an acoustic piano, it is also closest to the pedals and to the name of the piano maker.

Another good (and easy) note to remember is F: it is just to the left of the group of three black keys (see Figure 1.4).

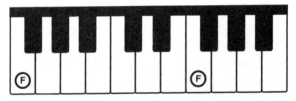

Figure 1.4 *An F is always just to the left of a group of three black keys.*

Now, to find D or E, all you have to do is count up from C (see Figure 1.5). To find G, you can count up from F. So to find A or B, you just keep counting up from G. Congratulations: you now know how to find all the white notes on the piano! (And pssst … you can count down, too, if you prefer.)

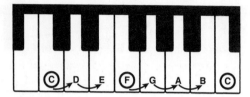

Figure 1.5 *From the notes you know, you can find the other notes by counting to the next letters.*

 Practice Makes Perfect

Try quizzing yourself about which note is which: Drop your hand on the piano and hit a note at random, then try to name it. Knowing which note is which will help you build chords later.

If you want to gain even more confidence in your note-naming ability, notice that every one of the seven notes in our musical alphabet occupies a unique place in relation to the surrounding black keys. For instance, D is always the white key in the middle of a group of two black keys. G is always the white key to the right of the first black key in a group of three black keys. Take a few minutes to study the keyboard, then close your eyes and feel a key. Try to identify it by feeling where it is in relation to groups of two or three black keys. Believe it or not, soon this will become second nature, and you'll recognize notes on a keyboard as easily as you recognize letters in the alphabet.

Ebony and Ivory

The five black notes take their names from the closest white notes. If you go up from a white note (to the right), the nearest black note is called a *sharp*, which is notated by a sign that looks like a tic-tac-toe board (#). If you go down from a white notes (to the left), the next black note is called a *flat*, which is noted like a slanty letter *b* (♭). See Figure 1.6 that follows.

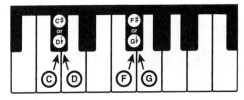

Figure 1.6   *Finding sharps and flats.*

So the black note that is to the right of middle C can be called either C# or D♭. The note to the right of F can be called F# or G♭.

Music professors have a long string of rules regarding whether they call a note a sharp or a flat, but to play a popular song, you don't really need to be concerned about that. All you need to remember is that a flat means go down to the very next key, and a sharp means go up to the very next key.

Music to Your Ears

Sharps and flats can also apply to white notes that have no black notes between them. So if you see an E# marked in the music, you find it by starting on E and going up to the very next note—which is an F because there is no black note between E and F. So F can be called E#. And E can be called Fb! This is rare, but it does happen.

Distances Between Notes

The distance between notes is measured in *steps* and *half steps*, also known as *intervals* (see Figure 1.7). A half step is the distance from one note to the very next note—whether it is a white note or a black note.

So the distance from a D to a D# is a half step, and the distance from a Gb to an F is a half step. The distance from an E to an F is also a half step— because there are no black notes between E and F.

A *whole step* is simply two half steps. A whole step can be from a white note to a white note, a black note to a black note, or a white note to a black note.

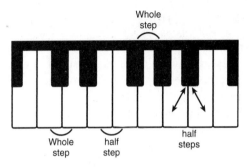

Figure 1.7 *Steps and half steps.*

Why do we care how far apart the notes are? Steps and half steps give us an easy way to talk to each other about which notes to play. In Chapter 4, you will learn that scales are groups of notes that go well together. Using half steps and steps helps us find the notes in a scale. Half steps and whole steps will also help us find the notes in chords.

 Universal Language

Intervals are distances between notes. A **half step** is the distance from one note to the very next note, regardless of whether it is a black note or white note. A **whole step** is two half steps. Practice finding steps and half steps on the piano. This will be essential when building chords.

Finger Placement

If you've ever taken classical piano lessons, you know that traditional teachers are obsessed with which finger goes on what key. Good fingering is essential for playing classical piano, but although it's helpful in popular piano, it's not as necessary. When you're starting out, it's useful to have a basic strategy of where to put which fingers. This helps prevent finger tangles, and helps you keep track of which note is which.

 Sour Notes

> Beginning piano players often jab at any old key with any old finger. Try to be consistent when you play a song: Your brain will learn faster if you always use the same fingers when you play any given series of notes.

In piano, fingers are numbered 1 through 5. The thumb is 1, the index finger is 2, the middle finger is 3, the ring finger is 4, and the pinky is 5.

To begin, the best strategy is to arrange your hand so that each finger is responsible for one note, and each note gets one finger. Try this on C: put your right-hand thumb on C, then each subsequent finger on each subsequent white note.

Practice Makes Perfect _____

Put the thumb of your right hand on C.
Each finger should sit on its own white
note. Play each finger in turn going up
and back down: 1-2-3-4-5-4-3-2-1. (You
should be playing C-D-E-F-G-F-E-D-C.) Then
move your hand so that your thumb is on
D and repeat the pattern. Move to E and
repeat the pattern. Repeat until your thumb
gets to the next C. Then try it with the left
hand: Starting on C with your left-hand
thumb, play 1-2-3-4-5-4-3-2-1. Continue
the exercise by moving down the keyboard to the next C.

A good basic hand position can also help you gain
control over your fingers. Your wrists should be
low and your fingers curved, so that you play with
the fingertips. (Professional pianists keep their nails
trimmed short.)

Don't be surprised or frustrated if some of your
fingers don't work as well as others, or if you have
trouble at first making each finger work independ-
ently. The practice suggestions in this book will
help you.

The Least You Need to Know

- The musical alphabet is made up of seven letters, from A to G. C is the white note just to the left of any group of two black notes.

- The distance between notes is measured in steps and half steps. A half step is from one note to its closest neighbor. A step (also called a whole step) is two half steps.

- Sharps mean that you play the note that is one half step higher; flats mean that you play the note that is one half step lower. Usually, sharps and flats will be black notes.

- Fingers are numbered 1 through 5, from the thumb to the pinky. It is easier to learn a song or a chord using a consistent, comfortable fingering.

2

Note Reading 101

In This Chapter

- Understanding a lead sheet
- Learning to read notes
- Reading sharps, flats, and other musical mysteries
- Discovering music notation for chords

Playing the piano using lead sheets and chord symbols requires only a minimum of note-reading ability—but without that minimum, you will be unable to learn new songs from a fake book. You might be able to learn the song by ear, but most adults taking up piano for the first time find it difficult to develop this skill. You might also be able to learn from a friend who shows you how the tune goes. But to learn a new song on your own, you need to read music.

A song is essentially made up of three parts. The melody is the tune—it's what you think of when you think about how the song goes. Harmony is the accompaniment. It's the part of the song that uses chords to give it depth and character. Rhythm is the beat—it's what makes you want to snap your fingers and tap your feet. The solo pianist needs to incorporate all three of these jobs. Without the melody, no one will know what song you are playing. Without harmony, the song sounds empty and unfinished. And without rhythm, no one will get up and dance.

In this chapter, you're going to learn enough about note reading to play the tune of a song. You'll also find music reading useful for learning new *riffs* and chord patterns from more advanced books.

 **Universal Language**

> A **riff** is a catchy or memorable pattern of notes that is usually repeated more than once, used to fill in empty spaces in a musical arrangement.

Anatomy of a Song

With traditional music, the composer gives you the exact notes written out for both the left hand and the right hand—which means that you've got to be able to read a ton of notes, all at the same time. With the chord approach, the composer gives you the notes in the tune and a set of instructions telling you which chords to play along with the tune. (See Figure 2.1.) It's not that you're playing any fewer notes. The difference is that you can play the chords any way you like, which removes a lot of the note-reading stress and offers you, as the performer, almost unlimited creativity.

Figure 2.1   *Lead sheet: The "C" over the line of music indicates that a C chord is to be played. The notes are the melody.*

You don't get a choice about the tune. Everyone knows how "You Are My Sunshine" goes, and if instead of the notes to "You Are My Sunshine," you start in on "Red River Valley," someone is likely to politely set you straight. So the first thing you need to do is be sure you can play the tune—otherwise, no one will know whether you're playing "Jingle Bells" or "Happy Birthday."

Reading Musical Hieroglyphics

You already know that as you move from left to right on the piano, the sound of the notes gets higher. If you move from right to left, the sound of the notes gets lower.

On a musical *staff*, notes also go up and down (see Figure 2.2). Notes are arranged on a musical staff consisting of five horizontal lines. Notes are represented by circles. These circles can either sit between the lines or they can sit on the lines. The higher the note's position on the staff, the higher it is on the keyboard. You read a line of music just like a book: from left to right.

Traditional piano music is written on two staffs, one for each hand. In a typical piano piece, the higher staff is used for the notes played by the right hand. It's also called the *G clef* or the *treble clef. Fake books* and *lead sheets* use the treble clef exclusively, because it's assumed that the melody will be played by the right hand.

Universal Language

A **fake book** contains a collection of **lead sheets,** in which the tune is written out in music notation and the accompaniment is indicated by chord symbols. Chord symbols are combinations of letters and numbers that tell you which chords to play. An arrangement is how you, as the performer, put together the melody and the chords to make a finished-sounding song.

A **staff** is a series of five lines on which notes are arranged. Space notes sit in the spaces between the lines. Line notes sit on the lines. The **treble clef,** also called the **G clef,** is usually played by the right hand. The **bass clef,** also called the **F clef,** is usually played by the left hand. The **grand staff** includes both the treble clef and the bass clef, and its two staves are linked together by a **brace,** which looks like a curvy bracket. **Ledger lines** are extra lines used above or below the main staff to add even higher or lower notes.

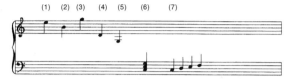

Figure 2.2   *(1) Right-hand space note (2) Right-hand line note (3) Right-hand high note (4) Right-hand low note (5) Right-hand note using ledger lines (6) Left-hand chord (7) Left-hand notes moving up the staff one step at a time.*

The squiggly G at the beginning of the line is a *G clef*, which tells you to play these notes with your right hand. The fraction is a time signature (see Chapter 3); it tells you how many beats there are in a measure. The vertical lines between some of the notes are bar lines, which group the notes into measures, each containing the same number of beats. Words may or may not be included in a lead sheet.

The *F clef*, also known as the *bass clef*, is used for the left hand. When you are playing from traditional sheet music, there will be two clefs joined together by a *brace*. This is called the *grand staff*. We won't be talking much about the bass clef in this book: the chord approach rarely uses it. But we do show you the notes on the bass clef, just in case you ever want to learn particular riffs or a bass line from sheet music.

Learning the Notes

How do you know which note is which? And do you really have to memorize 88 different piano keys?

Relax. I'm willing to bet that if you asked the best piano players you know to read the very lowest and the very highest notes on the piano, none of them could do it without counting lines and spaces.

You don't need to memorize all the notes—but you do need to learn a few. From those, you can count up or down to the notes you don't know. It's just like learning the names of the keys on the keyboard: you start with one or two that are easy to remember, and go on from there. Pretty soon, you'll find that you've memorized the notes you use all the time. And as for the low notes and high notes you don't use all the time—forget about them! If and when you need them, you'll know how to figure them out by counting the lines and spaces.

So let's get down to business. You've probably heard some variation of the old mnemonic "Every Good Boy Deserves Fudge." (Or Favor. Or Friends. Or that "Every Good Boy Does Fine." Use whichever you like.) The first letter of each of these words is the name of the notes on the lines of the treble clef, going from bottom to top: EGBDF. The word *FACE* is spelled by the names of the space notes on the treble clef.

If you're going to be reading notes in the left hand, you can also use memory aids to help find the notes. For the left-hand line notes, remember "Good Boys Deserve Fudge Always," which is GBDFA. "All Cows Eat Grass" gives you the names of the space notes: ACEG (see Figure 2.3).

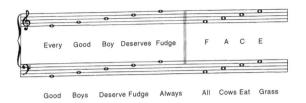

Figure 2.3

Music to Your Ears

The sign for the G clef is based on the medieval letter G. Notice that the swirl goes around the second line from the bottom of the staff. The G that is just above middle C "lives" on this line. Similarly, the sign for the F clef is based on the medieval letter F. It has two dots, located just above and just below the second line down from the top of the staff. The F that is just below middle C "lives" on this line.

Start by memorizing some easy-to-remember notes (see Figure 2.4). In addition to the F on the F clef and the G on the G clef, middle C is an easy note to recognize: it sits below the right-hand staff, and has a line going through its middle. High G is also easy because it sits right on top of the G clef's staff. (And low F hangs off the bottom of the F clef's staff.) Two other notes worth learning are the Cs that are above and below middle C.

The right-hand C is two spaces down from the top of the G clef; the left-hand C is two spaces up from the bottom of the F clef. If you can memorize and recognize these notes when you see them, it becomes easy to count up or down lines and spaces to nearby notes you haven't yet memorized.

Figure 2.4

Moving from Note to Note

So now that you know a few notes, how do you figure out the rest? The notes on the musical staff direct you to move up or down. But notes in a tune can be close together or far apart. So music notation also tells you how far to move up or down.

If we want to move up the keyboard from one note to the next, we move up the musical staff. If we start with a line note, the next note is the very next space note. If we start on a space note, we move to the very next line note. And so on.

If we skip one of these notes on the staff, we have to skip one on the piano. On a staff of music, skips are easy to see because the notes move from a line note to a line note (skipping a space note) or from a space note to a space note (skipping a line note). See Figure 2.5.

Stepping Up   Stepping Down   Skipping Up   Skipping Down   Big Skip Up

Figure 2.5

Skips can be any size: we can skip one note or many. If we skip more than one note, we count the lines and spaces in between the notes.

Learning Ledger Lines

If you're the kind of person who likes to analyze things, you might have noticed that there's one flaw with the musical staff we've been looking at: It doesn't have room for 88 notes. So what do you do, for example, if you want to play a note that is higher than the G that sits on top of the G clef?

When we run out of room on the staff, we add more lines on a temporary basis. These are called *ledger* lines. Let's say a composer wants us to play that high G, and then follow it with the A and the B just above it. The composer would write the G, and then follow it by drawing a ledger line for the A. The G is a space note, so the A would be a line note. (The ledger line goes right through its middle.) The B would be a space note, so it would sit on the ledger line.

The same procedure applies in the left hand to the low bass notes below the F, which is the lowest note on the F clef. Don't worry too much about these notes: in this book, we use the chord method, not note reading, for the left hand.

In a fake book with only one staff of music notation, you can also find ledger lines below the right-hand staff. Ledger lines are used if the right hand is going to be playing notes below middle C. Similarly, if the left hand is going to be playing notes above middle C, the composer has to draw ledger lines for these notes above the left-hand staff (see Figure 2.6).

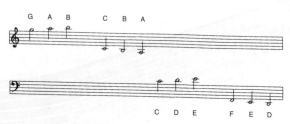

Figure 2.6

Sharps and Flats

You already know that sharps and flats are usually black notes, and that they are named after the white notes that are adjacent to them. You know that sharps mean to go up a half step, and flats mean to go down. And you know that a sharp sign looks a little like a tic-tac-toe board (#), and that a flat sign looks like an italicized letter *b* (♭). Sharp signs and flat signs are always written on the line or in the space that pertains to the note they go with.

Sharps and flats, along with the *natural* sign, which we'll get to in a minute, are called accidentals. There are three ways in which you will encounter accidentals in a piece of music.

First, you may see sharps or flats at the very beginning of the staff, before the music notation even starts. This is called a *key signature* (see Figure 2.7).

Figure 2.7   *Key signature showing one sharp (F#).*

Notice that there is one sharp at the very beginning of the line, right after the clef symbol. For music theory reasons, if there is only one sharp, it will invariably be on the "F" line, and it will mean that every F in the entire piece is to be played as an F sharp unless you are informed otherwise (more on that in a minute). A key signature can contain up to seven sharps or seven flats (although it is far more common to see one, two, or three sharps or flats in popular songs than it is to see seven!). The number of sharps or flats is called the key signature. Key signatures are explained in Chapter 4; in Appendix B, you will find a list of key signatures along with the names of the sharps and flats that go with them. For now, all you have to remember is if you see sharps or flats at the beginning of the staff, every note that is on those lines will be played as a sharp or a flat.

You may also see sharps or flats in front of individual notes. You are going along with no flats or sharps in sight, and suddenly you see a note with a sharp or flat in front of it. All you have to do is follow the directions: if it's a C with a sharp in front of it, you go up a half step and play C#. Sharps (and flats, too) are good for a whole measure. (We'll talk more about measures in Chapter 3, but for now, all you have to know is that a measure ends when you get to a vertical line, called a bar line, drawn through the staff.) If you see one C#, all the other Cs for the rest of the measure will also be C #. The bar line cancels the sharps: if the composer wants you to play a C# after the bar line, he has to tell you again.

You may see a natural sign ♮ in front of a note in the music. A natural sign cancels a sharp. Say you were playing a piece where every F was supposed to be an F#. But let's say that in the middle of the song, the composer suddenly wants the sound of a regular old F without the sharp. The composer would write a natural sign ♮ in front of that F, as if to say, "Wait! Sorry! Changed my mind!" A natural sign is good for a whole measure, too. See Figure 2.8 for examples of a sharp, flat, and natural.

A flat   A natural   A sharp

Figure 2.8

Music to Your Ears

When you're just starting out, look for songs without any sharps or flats in the key signature, because it's easier to play when you only have white notes to locate and play. A slow ballad is probably more manageable than an upbeat, syncopated rock tune. Folk tunes tend to be good starting-out choices. Leave the jazz till later.

Music Notation for Chords

When you're reading music, you read left to right, just like a book. Notes to be played at the same time are stacked up on top of each other. This isn't something you'll see in lead sheets, which just contain a melody and chord symbols. But it is something you'll see in sheet music, and we're going to take a quick look at how chords are notated so you have the tools you need to be able to use other resources as you learn to play.

In their simplest rendition (and yes, there are tons of not-so-simple renditions) chords look a little like snowmen: three circles (notes) stacked up on top of each other (see Figure 2.9). Because we're going to be playing our chords with the left hand, we'll use the bass clef.

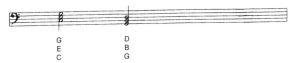

G   D
E   B
C   G

Figure 2.9 *How chords look: the C chord and G chord in their most basic arrangement.*

Notice that the first chord is made up of a stack of all space notes. Let's find the first one on the keyboard. Using your left hand, find the starting (bottom) note with your pinky. In this case, that's the C below middle C. The next note is a space note, which means that you skip the D and play an E with your third finger. Then, you skip the F and play the G with your thumb (see Figure 2.10).

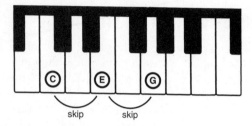

Figure 2.10 *Playing the C chord.*

The second chord starts on G. (You'll have to move your whole hand down so that the pinky is on G.) You then skip A, play B with your third finger, skip C, and play D with your thumb (see Figure 2.11).

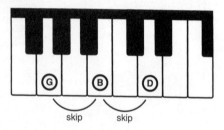

Figure 2.11 *Playing the G chord.*

Being able to read chords—by figuring out what each note is, one at a time, then playing them together—is a good skill to develop, because it lets you read left-hand riffs that may be difficult to figure out by ear (such as the left-hand patterns in Chapter 8). But you don't have to worry about being fluent at it. In the rest of this book, you learn how to construct chords based on their symbols. We won't be reading them at all.

The Least You Need to Know

- Music is written with notes on a musical staff comprising five lines.
- The G clef is used for right-hand notes, and the F clef is used for left-hand notes.
- As you move higher on the musical staff, the notes get higher, and as you move lower, the notes get lower.
- The key signature tells you how many sharps and how many flats you will be using as you play the song.
- In sheet music, chords are indicated by three or more notes stacked on top of each other.

Chapter 3

You've Got Rhythm

In This Chapter

- Finding the beat
- Reading rhythmic notation
- Understanding chords and rhythm

There's one more aspect to reading music that you need to understand before we can truly get into the swing of things. Rhythm is almost impossible to define—but you know when you've got it. (And you sure know when someone doesn't have it, don't you?)

Rhythm is the aspect of music that makes you tap your feet, get up and dance, snap your fingers, or shake whatever it is that you might want to shake. An audience often doesn't notice your wrong notes, but they'll notice if you lose the beat. A break in the rhythm feels like you're being jolted around in a car driven by someone who can't operate the stick shift.

This chapter discusses the two aspects of rhythm that pianists are most concerned about: how to read rhythm notation so the melody sounds right, and how rhythm and chords work together.

Rhythm and Melody

Rhythm can make or break an entire song. To see how, simply go to your piano and, starting on C (any C) and going down, play every white note down to the next C.

Doesn't sound like much, does it? Try it again. It doesn't sound like much of a tune.

What if I told you that those exact notes, in that exact order, were the notes that begin one of the most popular Christmas carols ever? Want proof? Play these notes again, but this time, think of the song "Joy to the World." Try to match what you're playing to the tune you hear in your head. Sing as you play to remind yourself of how the song goes. Which notes are long and which are short? Now you have a whole different, instantly recognizable tune.

Music notation not only tells you which note to play, but how long to hold it. It is the combination of long notes, short notes, and medium notes— a sort of musical Morse code—that gives music rhythm. When you play a song with the long notes and the short notes in the right places, the audience can recognize the tune and clap along.

An exact reading of music notation is not necessary for playing popular music. When you start out, you'll probably choose songs you already know—and this means that you will most likely be playing most of the rhythms at least partly by ear. After all, you didn't have sheet music in front of you when you sang "Joy to the World," yet you managed to get the long notes and the short notes in all the right places. In the same way, when your fingers can find the notes to a tune you've heard before, you will almost automatically play the long and short notes in approximately the right places. However, to play music you haven't heard before, you need to know how to read rhythmic notation.

Another thing to remember is that improvising is at the heart of the chord method—and that includes rhythm. The fact that you are improvising doesn't give you permission to play any old note you want anywhere; the audience still has to recognize the song. But it does give you some leeway.

Finding the Beat

The beat is probably the most important part of rhythm. You can change around some of the notes if you like (especially when you become more skilled). But you absolutely must get the right number of beats to a *measure*.

 Universal Language _____

A **measure** contains notes grouped in a repeating number of beats according to the time signature.

Think of the beat as the regular repeating sound that makes you want to clap your hands. Think of the old song, "She'll Be Coming Round the Mountain." Sing it to yourself.

If you can see yourself clapping to this, you know what a beat is. If you can hear yourself counting to four as you're clapping, and then counting to four again, you already understand how rhythmic counting works.

Still not sure about counting beats? Put on a CD—anything that makes you want to dance or clap. As you're listening, start to clap. You don't need a search party to find the beat, or even any real musical talent. All you have to do is listen and when you feel the beat, start clapping. Every time you clap, that is one beat.

Now start counting. Obviously, you're not going to count to 100 or 1,000 or however many beats there are in the whole entire song! That would be unwieldy, not to mention useless. Instead, count to a number that feels right—usually three or four (unless you're listening to something really unusual). Then go back to one and start all over again. If you're counting to a rock 'n' roll tune, chances are you're counting to four. If you're counting to a waltz, you're counting to three.

Play what you count, don't count what you play. When you learn a song, count in your head (or, even better, out loud). Tapping your foot helps, too. Try to make your counting as even as a *metronome*. Many beginners speed up when they are confident and slow down when they feel shaky, which usually results in learning incorrect rhythms. Wrong rhythms stick in your brain like chewing gum on a shoe; they can be fiendishly difficult to unlearn. So try to play in strict time, even if you have to play slowly or scramble to find some of the notes.

 Universal Language

> A **metronome** is a device that ticks—like a loud grandfather clock—in strict time. You can think of a metronome as a really boring but totally dependable drummer. The purpose is to give you a steady beat to play along with. Metronomes can be electronic or wind-up. Many electronic keyboards also have built-in metronomes.

Time Signatures

Each group of beats (usually three beats or four beats) is grouped together in a measure. A measure is indicated in music notation as a vertical line (also called a *bar line*) cutting across the staff. The time signature tells you how many beats there are in a measure. This is important: if you know the number of beats, you can fake your way through anything. If you don't, you're as lost as a fish on the moon. In the vast majority of cases, there will be either three beats or four beats to a measure, and this will be consistent throughout the song. (As always, exceptions exist, but we can safely ignore them for now.) What this means in plain English is that you count to four (or three), and then you count to four (or three) again, and you give each beat the exact same amount of time as every other beat.

The time signature is usually expressed as a fraction at the beginning of the piece. In the simpler time signatures (which is all we're going to deal with here), the top note tells you how many beats there are in the measure. The bottom note tells you which kind of note "gets the beat"—in other words, the bottom number tells you which kind of note you would clap on.

Music to Your Ears

Most musicians are content to play in typical time signatures, which usually involves counting to either three or four in a measure. But Dave Brubeck's 1959 classic "Take Five" is entirely in the time signature of $\frac{5}{4}$, meaning that you count to five when you're counting the beats.

$\frac{4}{4}$ (also written c) is by far the most commonly used time signature. It means that there are four quarter notes in a measure, and you would clap on each one. $\frac{3}{4}$ is the second most commonly used signature.

It indicates that there are three quarter notes in a measure, and you would clap on each one.

Reading Note Values

If you're playing a tune you already know, it may be enough to just read the notes and feel your way through the rhythm. But what if you want to play a song you've never played before? Well, then you're going to have to understand how the long notes and the short notes are written (see Figure 3.1).

(1)   (2)   (3)   (4)   (5)   (6)

Figure 3.1 *The different ways of writing a note shows you how long to hold it.*

Reading rhythm starts with recognizing that the way a note is written tells you how long to hold it. We don't measure that time period in seconds; we measure it in beats. For example …

- A quarter note, written as a note filled with solid black, gets one beat.
- A half note is an empty note with a stem. It gets two beats, which means that after you play it you hold it while you count to two.
- A dot after a note adds half the value of that note. So a dotted half note gets three beats (two beats for the half note, plus one beat for the dot).

- A whole note, written as an empty circle, gets four beats.

- A dotted quarter consists of a quarter note followed by a dot. It gets one and a half beats: One beat for the quarter note plus one half beat for the dot.

- Tied notes are linked together with a curvy line. They get the sum total of the two notes that are tied together; the note is played only once.

Beats can also be subdivided. To see how, clap and count: 1-2-3-4. Now continue counting one number per clap, but this time squeeze the word *and* in between: 1-and-2-and-3-and-4-and. Those are eighth notes: You're getting two notes for each clap, or two eighth notes for each quarter note.

Eighth notes can be further subdivided into sixteenths and even smaller values. This is just a matter of simple math: If there is one whole note in a measure, there could also be two half notes, or four quarter notes, or eight eighth notes, or sixteen sixteenth notes, and so on. Of course, the smaller the time value of the note, the faster you have to play it!

Triplets means that the rhythm is divided so that it has a 1-2-3 feel. You can count triplets 1-and-a 2-and-a 3-and-a (see Figure 3.2).

COUNT: 1 + 2 + 3 + 4 +   1 + a 2 + a 3 + a 4 + a

Figure 3.2 *Count "1-and" for eighth notes and "1-and-a" for triplets.*

Other symbols you'll see are rests, which can be thought of as place holders. There's no note being played, but the silence takes up a certain amount of space (see Figure 3.3).

(1)   (2)   (3)   (4)

Figure 3.3 *The different types of rests indicate a period of silence. The length of the silence depends on the type of rest.*

Different types of rests take up different numbers of beats. For example …

1. A whole rest is a solid rectangle that hangs off of one of the lines of the staff. It takes up the whole measure; it can be used for four beats or three beats, depending on the time signature.

2. A half rest is a solid rectangle that sits on top of one of the lines of the staff and takes up two beats.

3. A quarter rest looks a little like a drawing of a lightning strike and takes up one beat.

4. An eighth rest looks a little like a stylized numeral "7" and takes up half of a beat.

Rhythm and Chords

Okay, so you've got the melody down, and now you want to play chords. In Chapter 2, we looked at how chords appear when they are written out in sheet music. If you're playing from a fake book, you'll just be given the chord symbol. Either way, you have to know—or decide—when to play the chord. (We'll talk about building different chords throughout the rest of the book.)

Let's go back and play that C chord you learned to read in Chapter 2 (C-E-G). Play it with your left hand starting on the C below middle C. Your pinky goes on that low C, your third finger goes on E, and your thumb goes on G. Some people have trouble playing three notes while holding the other two fingers up. Play this chord several times to get the feel of it.

The easiest way to start playing songs with chords is to choose songs that have only one chord per measure. This gives you plenty of time to coordinate your hands, and, if necessary, move between chords. The first line of "Jingle Bells" (see Figure 3.4) is a good place to practice playing chords in rhythm with the melody because there is only one chord—the C chord you already know.

In the first two measures of this example, there is only one chord per measure. That means you would play the chord on the first beat of each measure at the same time you play the first melody note in each measure. Then, while you continue to play the melody with the right hand, you hold the chord down for the entire measure.

Figure 3.4   *Sheet music for the first line of "Jingle Bells."*

In the third measure there are two chords, each written as half notes. This means that you play the chord twice. You play it on the first beat (with the melody note that goes with the first syllable of the *Jingle* in "Jingle all the way"). And you play the chord again on the word *all*. You finish the line by playing one last chord on the word *way* and holding it for four beats.

In Chapter 8, we suggest left-hand patterns that will help give your playing a strong rhythmic feel and more interest. For now, it is enough to get your left hand and your right hand playing together, and to stress steadiness and repetition. Every strong rhythmic groove is based on an easily identified pattern being repeated over and over.

Changing Chords

If you look at a lead sheet, you'll see that the chord symbols above the melody notes change every once in a while (see Figure 3.5). These new chord symbols tells you to stop playing the old chord and start playing a different chord. It is most common for these changes to take place on the first beat of a measure, but they can also take place on a different beat, in which case the new chord will be written right over the note it goes with.

Figure 3.5   *The second line of "Jingle Bells."*

In the last line of "Jingle Bells," you change chords on every measure. You learned to read and play two of these chords in Chapter 2. A reminder: the notes for the C chord are C-E-G, and the notes for the G chord are G-B-D. The F chord is new: it uses the notes F-A-C. (Put your left-hand pinky on the F, your left-hand middle finger on A, and your left-hand thumb on C.) Practice playing the melody with your right hand alone a few times, then play these three chords a few times with your left hand alone. When both hands are comfortable, put them together. The left hand should play each chord on the first beat of each measure.

The key to playing these *changes* (as jazz musicians call a series of chords) is to practice them until the transitions are smooth and you can move from one to the other without hesitating. That's when you know you've taken the first step to playing "in the groove."

The Least You Need to Know

- Rhythm is the organization of long notes and short notes that makes a listener want to clap along.

- Rhythmic notation shows the relative duration of notes in a song.

- Finding and keeping a steady beat is the musician's number-one priority.

- Beats are grouped into measures, and each measure (almost always) has the same number of beats as all the others in a tune.

- Chords played in strong repeated rhythms can help establish a groove for a song.

Chapter 4

Building Chords with Do-Re-Mi

In This Chapter

- Building a five-note scale
- Finding the notes in a major chord
- Playing one chord several ways
- Making an eight-note scale

We've finally reached the heart of the matter: chords, which provide the harmony, or accompaniment, for a piece. Chords are clusters of notes. They can be played either all at the same time or with their notes broken up into a regular, repeating pattern. Chords give a song depth and character, and can evoke agitation, excitement, serenity, and a thousand other emotions. They turn a simple tune you can whistle into a song to remember. But how do you know which notes to play?

The two-word answer to this question is "music theory"—words that most people put on a par with such pleasures as high school physics or a trip to the dentist. But before you trade in your piano for a drum set, hold on a minute! Music theory may be the most erroneously named concept in all of music: it's like calling a Labrador retriever "Killer." There is absolutely nothing theoretical about music theory. Music theory should be called music reality. What it does is tell you, clearly and simply, how music works.

Scales: Music's "Secret Decoder Ring"

Now that I've reassured you about music theory, I'm going to introduce another word that strikes terror into the hearts of former music students. *Scales.* Okay, there, I said it. But here, too, what looks at first glance like an ogre turns out to be just another puppy. A scale is really nothing more than a series of notes that sound good together.

Now when I say scales, I don't mean that you have to spend hours zipping up and down the piano, nor will the piano-teacher police swoop down to enforce their fingering laws. Think of scales instead as a secret decoder ring. Scales reveal patterns that help you find the notes to make any chord on the whole piano.

Making a Chord

Chords come in many shapes and sizes (literally): They can be complex or simple, consonant or dissonant, obvious or oblique. We're not going to start with the hardest, weirdest jazz chord you've ever heard. We're going to start simple, with a three-note chord known as a *major triad*—the same kind of chord you played in "Jingle Bells."

Universal Language

A triad is a three-note chord. Different kinds of triads have different kinds of sounds, which are sometimes characterized as happy or sad (although that probably has more to do with the kinds of songs we associate them with than with any inherent happiness or sadness in the chords themselves). In this chapter, we discuss the basic **major triad**, which most people associate with a happy sound. Other triads are discussed in Chapter 6.

To make our major chord, we'll start with a five-note scale. And don't get all freaked out, because you already know a five-note scale. I snuck it into Chapter 1, while you were busy with steps and half steps. You played it when you put your right-hand thumb on C and played each finger up to G and back down again. Go back to your piano and try it again. C-D-E-F-G. Remember to use one finger for each note: 1-2-3-4-5.

This five-note scale has a very distinct sound. Remember the "Do-Re-Mi-Fa-Sol-La-Ti-Do" scale from the *The Sound of Music*? Our five-note scale contains the first five notes of this Do-Re-Mi scale. Go ahead and sing as you play.

The Scale Method

So how do you turn a five-note scale into a three-note chord? By playing three of its notes: the first note of your five-note scale, the third note, and the fifth note. If you're playing with your right hand, play C with your thumb, E with your third finger, and G with your pinky. Now play them all at the same time. Congratulations! You've just built your first chord! (And if it sounds familiar, that probably means you've been practicing "Jingle Bells" because this is the very same chord we read in Chapter 2 and played in Chapter 3.)

The five-note scale can be used to make a major triad starting on any note on the piano, but before you try to do that, you need a little more information.

 **Sour Notes**

To practice five-note scales, designate one finger per note. Be especially careful when you get to scales with black notes: your fingers may tend to slide off the key they are supposed to play. If necessary, say the note names as you play them: This brings your brain in line with your fingers. If your fingers start migrating from note to note, you will end up playing chords that don't, to put it mildly, belong in choirs of angels.

Try playing a five-note scale starting on D and going up to A, using only white notes. Put the thumb of your right hand on D, then play 1-2-3-4-5. (You'll be playing D-E-F-G-A.) Do this a few times so you can play it easily: you want to be able to concentrate on how it sounds.

If you have a keen ear, you'll notice that this all-white-note five-note scale starting on the D doesn't have the same sound as the all-white-note five-note scale starting on C. If you had to characterize the difference, you might say that the scale starting on D sounds a little sadder, or more somber, than the scale starting on C. That's because the arrangement of white keys and black keys is different when you start on different notes. To make a true Do-Re-Mi scale starting on D, you need to make some adjustments, and this means adding black notes.

Practice Makes Perfect

Put your ears to work as you make your scales and chords. A wrong note will probably sound wrong to you, so listen carefully. If something sounds off, try adjacent notes and listen to how they sound.

How do you figure out how many black notes to add to your D scale? Or which ones? We use intervals—those steps and half steps we learned about in Chapter 1. No matter which note you start on, the distance between the notes in any five-note major scale is always the same. The key thing to remember is that it doesn't matter whether a note is black or white. All that matters is the distance between them. Let's see how this works by going back to our five-note scale starting on C (see Figure 4.1).

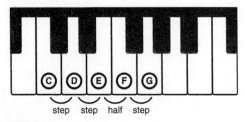

Figure 4.1 *The distance between C and D is a whole step. D to E is another whole step. E to F is a half step. F to G is a whole step.*

Now let's start on D and use the exact same pattern of half steps and whole steps (see Figure 4.2). We will get a five-note do-re-mi scale, but it will have one black note in it.

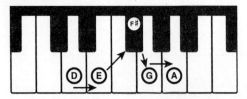

Figure 4.2 *From D, go up a whole step to E. Next, go up another whole step to F# (a black note). From F#, we move up a half step to G. From G, we move up a whole step to A.*

And now that you've found your D five-note scale, you know how to play a D chord: just play the first, third, and fifth notes of the scale. That's D, F#, and A. Voilà!

Practice Makes Perfect _____

Go up and down the keyboard and find five-note scales beginning on the following notes: G, D, A, F, B♭, and E♭. The half-step, whole-step pattern should always be the same: play the starting note, then go up a whole step, go up another whole step, go up a half step, go up a whole step. Playing the first, third, and fifth note of any major five-note scale gives you the major chord.

And that's all there is to it: you now know how to make a five-note scale on any note. And, by playing the first, third, and fifth notes of a five-note scale, you also know how to make a major chord on any note.

The Step Method

There are actually two ways to make a chord, and most pianists switch back and forth between chord-building methods depending on the scale and the type of chord. The step method is based on the intervals (distances between notes) that you learned in Chapter 1. Many pianists find this method easier in some situations. To see how the step method works, let's go back to our C chord (C-E-G).

We are trying to figure out the distance between the bottom note of the chord and the middle note of the chord, and the distance between the middle note of the chord and the top note of the chord. Going note by note, starting on C, the distance from C to E is two whole steps. (C to C# is a half step, C to D is two half steps, C to D# is 3 half steps. So the distance from C to E is four half steps [or two whole steps].)

We do the same thing to figure out the distance from the second note of the chord (E) to the third note of the chord (G). Counting up from E, we come to F (one half step), F# (two half steps), and G (three half steps). The distance from E (the second note of the C chord) to G (the top note of the C chord) is three half steps, or a step and a half (see Figure 4.3).

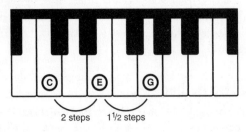

2 steps   1½ steps

Figure 4.3 *Measuring steps between notes in a C chord.*

The distance from the first note of a major chord to the second note of a major chord is always four half steps (or two whole steps). And the distance from the second note to the third note is always three half steps (or, if you prefer, "a step and a half").

Practice Makes Perfect

Your left hand is going to be doing most of the chord playing, so be sure it gets plenty of practice time. Try playing your five-note scales and chords rhythmically with the left hand. Starting with your pinky on C, play the five-note scale and then the C chord. Move up to D and do the same thing, then E, and so on up through the white notes. When you can play the scales and chords on all the white notes, start on the black notes and do the same thing.

Variations on a Chord

You now know how to make a major triad on any note. You've played your chords a few times, and they sound pretty good. But you know that it can't be that simple: Ray Charles, Elton John, and Bill Evans didn't just play the same chord over and over. Or did they? Well, yes and no. In many cases, the most elegant arrangements of songs are the simplest ones. But it's also true that good pianists move all over the keyboard. After you get comfortable with the notes in any given chord, you can start experimenting with other ways to play it.

Let's go back to our trusty C chord. We know that a C chord consists of the notes C-E-G. But here's a little piece of information that will immediately spice up your playing: there are no limitations regarding which notes you play. You can play any C on the whole piano, any E, and any G—in any order, anywhere you like. Go ahead and experiment: Try playing a G down low and a C up high and an E in the middle. Don't like the sound of that? Put the E down low, the C up high, and the G in the middle. Arranging the notes of a chord in a way that sounds good to you is called *voicing*. All that is required is that you play the notes in the chord. (And in advanced jazz playing, even this rule gets bent. But we'll talk about that in Chapter 9.) Where you play them is up to you.

Another way to vary a chord is to turn it upside down. This is called an *inversion*. The C chords we've been making with our five-note scale have all been in *root position* so far, meaning that in a C chord, C is the lowest note, and all the other notes follow in order. (E is the middle note, and G is the highest note.) Go ahead and play your C chord with middle C as the lowest note.

To invert the chord, you're simply going to take the note that is on the bottom and put it on the top. So keep playing the same E and the same G. But instead of playing middle C again, play the C that is one octave higher than middle C. (This will entail moving your hand.) Your chord now contains E-G-C. These are all notes in the C chord—the only difference is that the note that was on the bottom is now on the top. This is called *first inversion*.

You can invert the chord again by moving the E (which is now the lowest note of the chord) up an octave (making E the highest note of the chord). See Figure 4.4. Your chord now contains G-G-E, which are still the notes of the C chord, but in a different order. This is called *second inversion*.

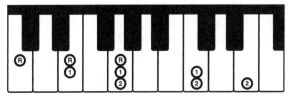

Figure 4.4 *C chord inversions. Notes noted "R" are in root position. Notes noted "1" are in first inversion. Notes noted "2" are in the second inversion. In each case, we have taken the note that was on the bottom and moved it one octave higher.*

Universal Language _____

The **root** is the name of the chord. **Voicing** a chord means choosing the order in which to play its three notes. An **inversion** is a way of playing a chord where you take the bottom note of the chord and put it on the top. **Root position** means that the notes of the chord are arranged in order and the root is the lowest note.

For now, it's enough to know two things about inversions: that chords can be played all over the piano, and that inversions will (believe it or not) make playing the piano much easier when you start moving from one chord to another. (We talk about that in Chapter 5.)

The Full Do-Re-Mi Scale

Thus far, we've only dealt with the five-note scale. But what about those other notes? After all, the Do-Re-Mi scale doesn't actually stop at Sol—it goes all the way from Do up to another Do. Go ahead and sing it. Do-Re-Mi-Fa-Sol-La-Ti-Do.

This complete Do-Re-Mi scale is also called the *major scale.* Later, when you build more complex chords, you're going to be using it to find more notes to add to your chords.

Making the Major Scale

To make a complete major scale, we start with our five-note scale. The five-note C scale contained C-D-E-F-G. Our full C major scale contains these exact same notes, but it continues to A (up a whole step from G), then B (up another whole step), and it ends on C (up a half step). See Figure 4.5.

Just as with the five-note scales, the whole trick to constructing a full Do-Re-Mi scale is to get the right arrangement of steps and half steps between the notes. Try making a full major scale on another note, say, E (see Figure 4.6).

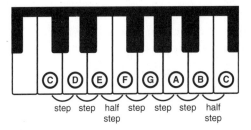

Figure 4.5 *The whole-step, half-step pattern for the major scale is this: root-whole-whole-half-whole-whole-whole-half.*

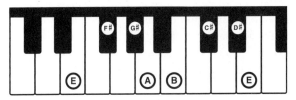

Figure 4.6 *Major scale starting on E. E-F# is a step; F#-G# is a step; G#-A is a half step; A-B is a step; B-C# is a step, C-D# is a step; D#-E is a half step.*

Scales and Key Signatures

As you've been making your five-note scales and your complete Do-Re-Mi scales, you've undoubtedly noticed that some have no black notes, some have one black note, and some have several black notes. There seems to be no rhyme or reason to which black and white notes you use. But there is!

In Chapter 2, you learned that seeing a number of sharps or flats at the beginning of a line of music tells you that every time you see one of those notes in the music, you are to play it as a sharp or a flat.

These sharps and flats at the beginning of a piece have another purpose, too: they also help you figure out which key the piece is in.

When musicians talk about "keys," they're not wondering where they put their car keys. "We're going to do blues in A," a musician might say, and believe it or not, that's all the band needs to hear to jam all night. The fact that it's a blues tune tells the musicians which types of chords they'll be needing and which order they'll play them in. (We show you how this works in Chapter 8.) The key identifies which specific chords and which groups of notes they can improvise with. Not all musical styles are as predictable as the blues. But even in a complex song, knowing what key you're in tells you which notes and chords you'll be using most of the time.

Music to Your Ears _____

Correct fingering for scales is important if you plan to play scales. (You can buy scale exercise books that show these fingerings in any store that carries sheet music.) Playing scales increases your technical facility and is useful for right-hand improvising. But for now, it's perfectly okay to use just your index finger to pick out the notes of a scale—or whatever fingering you feel comfortable with.

So what does it mean to "be in a key"? Think of the key you're in as home base. In music, it's also called the *tonic*. You can think of a song as a journey: starting out from the home key (a place of stability), going away, either to a nearby familiar place (a closely related key) or to a faraway place (a more distant key), then returning home.

This idea of a home key in music is a very powerful one. To see how it works, play the last line of "Jingle Bells" again. But instead of playing the whole last line, stop on the second-to-last note, just before you would sing *sleigh* in "one-horse open sleigh." There's a feeling of incompletion, isn't there? Try playing the song this way to a young child: stop before the word *sleigh* and dollars to donuts, your little musical genius will finish the song for you. The pull toward that last note is so strong that it's impossible to let the song end on the second-to-last note. You need to finish it. That last note is the "key you're in." When you finally do sing *sleigh*, you know you're done, and so does your audience.

Being in a key tells you where home base is: it's the song's point of stability. When you played "Jingle Bells," you were in the key of C: the C note and the C chord were your ending notes and your point of stability. And the notes you used in the melody were taken from the C scale.

Each key has its own unique combination of black notes and white notes—its key signature. You don't have to memorize key signatures right away, although you will probably want to at some point. Appendix B shows the names of all the keys, and tells you how many sharps or flats each key has and which ones they are.

Scale Degrees

There is another way to think of the notes in the scale: by numbers instead of letters. Now why on earth would we want to do that? Doesn't it just make everything more complicated? Actually, the opposite is true.

To see why, let's remember how we made our first chords. You formed your five-note C scale, then you played the chord by playing the first note, the third note, and the fifth note. In musician number-speak, we made the chord by playing the 1, the 3, and the 5. And those instructions work for every other chord on any other note, so when we moved into a new key (D), we made our five-note scale again—and then we made our D chord by playing the 1, the 3, and the 5.

Basically, thinking in terms of numbers means that whenever you are in a key, you know what the first note of the scale is, and the second note, and the third note, and so on. That's all there is to it. This becomes useful when dealing with more complex chords, whose formulas include numbers that you will have to add to your basic triad. We cover this in Chapters 7 and 9.

Minor Scales

There are many kinds of scales: in addition to the standard major scale we've been talking about, there are minor scales, blues scales, modal scales, and a whole bunch of others—and to be honest, most of them you really don't need to know.

You do need to know what minor scales are, because it's common for songs to be played in minor keys. Each major key has a sister minor key. This minor key starts on a different note than the major scale, but otherwise contains exactly the same notes (and the same number of sharps and flats) as the major key (see Figure 4.7). No matter what major key you're in, its relative minor will always be one and half steps down from the tonic. Or you can think of the relative minor as starting on the sixth degree of the major scale.

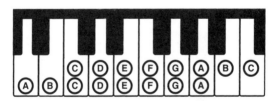

Figure 4.7 *The upper circles show the notes in the C major scale. The lower notes show the notes in the A minor scale.*

To hear the difference between a major scale and a minor scale, start on A instead of C and play all the white notes from A up to the next A. We'll discuss more about minor chords in subsequent chapters.

The Least You Need to Know

- A five-note scale always uses the same pattern of steps and half steps between the notes.

- Chords can be made from the first, third, and fifth notes of any five-note scale.

- Notes can be referred to by numbers, or degrees, which indicate where they are in any given scale.

- Major scales sound like the Do-Re-Mi-Fa-Sol-La-Ti-Do scale you may already be familiar with.

- Every major scale has a relative minor scale that uses the same notes.

Chapter 5

One Progression, Thousands of Songs

In This Chapter

- Determining which chords go with which other chords
- Using the "Circle of Fifths"
- Understanding chord numbers and why you need them
- Discovering the most popular progression in popular music
- Learning easy ways to play sequences of chords

The simple triad that you learned to create in Chapter 3 is the foundation of literally hundreds of chords and a world of harmony. But although there are scores of chords to choose from, the fact is that most songs have only a handful of them. Not only that, but chords tend to occur in combinations that are very predictable, after you know the rules.

So although there are enough chords to keep you amused, intrigued, delighted, and confused for the foreseeable future, you don't have to know them all. Countless songs, including the vast majority of folk songs and blues songs and many popular and rock 'n' roll songs as well, have only three chords. Thousands more songs have four or five chords, but these, too, follow predictable patterns. Although complicated jazz tunes do contain more chords, these chords tend to be based on the same predictable patterns.

In this chapter, we look at the most common combination of chords in popular music. We also look at which chords typically go with which other chords, and give you some practice and playing tips that will put them at your fingertips more quickly.

Cliques of Chords

We start with the key signature. In Chapter 4, you learned what it means to "be in a key" and that each key has its own combination of sharps and flats. (For which sharps and flats go with which key, see Appendix B.) Knowing what key you're in helps in a couple of ways. First off, it tells you which sharps and flats you're likely to encounter, which helps when you're struggling through a new melody. Second, knowing the key you're in also tells you which combinations of notes will sound good to improvise with. And of most use to us right now, it tells you which chords you'll be likely to play.

Why? Because keys are a lot like cliques. Remember high school? The guys on the football team didn't usually hang out with the guys on the debate team. The chords in the C major clique don't usually hang around with the chords in the F# clique. They just don't have a lot in common.

Why do we care which chords hang out with which other chords? Because thinking in patterns makes music easier to play. Musicians playing a song in the key of C major know that they're likely to see a lot of C, F, and G chords. (We'll get to how they know this in a minute.) So instead of worrying about having to be ready to play 100 different chords, musicians who know what key they're playing in know where their hands are going to be headed, at least most of the time.

How do you know what key a song is in? Start by checking the key signature. (Refer to the key signature chart in Appendix B, or to the Circle of Fifths.) In the key of C, there are no sharps or flats.

Sour Notes

Don't forget that each major key has a related minor key that has the same number of sharps or flats! One good way to tell whether a song is in C major or A minor is to check out the last chord in the song. If it's a C, chances are good that the song is in C. If it's an Am, the tune is probably in A minor.

So now that we know how to figure out which key we're in, how do we know which chords hang out with which other chords? An ingenious little device called the Circle of Fifths literally puts all the scales and their related chords at your fingertips (see Figure 5.1).

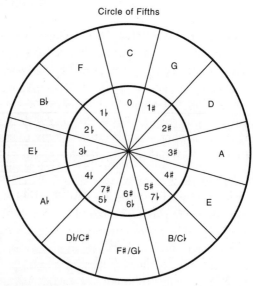

Circle of Fifths

outside circle is major key
middle circle is relative minor key
inner circle is number of sharps or flats

Figure 5.1 *Circle of Fifths.*

First, some reassurance: although some musicians see the Circle of Fifths as a delightful puzzle, others look at it and scratch their heads in be-fuddlement. The important thing to remember is that, just as you don't have to be an architect to

live in a house, you do not have to understand the
theory behind the Circle of Fifths to use it. The
important thing is that it contains some information you need. First, it tells you at a glance how
many sharps or flats each key has. And second, it
tells you which chords you're most likely to be
using when you are playing in any given key.

The Circle of Fifths and Chord Progressions

What the Circle of Fifths does is tell you how
closely related one key is to another—and how
closely related various chords are. Keys and chords
that are right next to each other on the Circle are
closely related. Keys clear on the other side of the
Circle are distantly related.

In any key, the most closely related chords—and
hence, the most commonly used—are the chords
immediately next door on the Circle of Fifths.
Suppose you're playing a song in C. The tonic
chord is C. The chord immediately clockwise is
the G chord, and the chord immediately counterclockwise is the F chord. These are the chords that
are the head honchos in the C major clique.

Want to know the most common chords in the
key F sharp? Simple: go to F sharp. (Notice that
it can also be called G flat. This is just something
that happens when keys have a lot of sharps or
flats.) The chord to the clockwise side is C#.
The chord to the counterclockwise side is B. These
chords, along with F#, of course, are the primary
chords in the key of F#.

Chord Numbers

In Chapter 3, we talked about scales and how each note in a scale could be referred to by a number.

With chords, we use numbers, too—but we use Roman numerals. As it turns out, the primary chords in any key (the chords we identified as being next door on the Circle of Fifths) are also always the chords that start on the first note of the scale, the fourth note on any scale, and the fifth note of any scale. We call these chords the I, the IV, and the V. In C, the first note is C so the C chord is the I chord. The fourth note of the C scale is F, so the F chord is the IV chord. The fifth note of the C scale is G, so the G chord is the V chord.

The chords that "belong" to a scale are built starting on a note in the scale, and using only notes that are in the scale. The C chord is built on the first degree of the C scale, so it is called the I chord. It contains the C-E-G, which are all notes in the C scale. The F chord (the IV) contains F-A-C, also all in the C scale. And the G chord (the V chord) contains G-B-D—also in the C scale.

What does all this mean in terms of actual music? A song in any key will mostly be using melody notes taken from that scale. The chords in that key will also use notes taken from its scale.

Okay, I admit, that drum set might be looking like a pretty good alternative to the piano right about now. But chord numbers—after you learn them— are another one of those complicated-sounding music theory things that make playing easier. Numbers give us information that is essential for improvisers and chord players—especially people who accompany others or who play in bands.

Music to Your Ears _____

Don't worry if you see chords that have notes that are not in the key of the song. This is called modulating, or moving from one key to another. Basically, you begin the song in one key, then modulate, or move, to another key for a while—and then you come back home to the original key. Simply think of it as a slightly more interesting musical journey.

They also give us a key piece of information: the identities of the most common chords in popular music, the I, IV, and V chords, which make up the most common progression in music. There are many more progressions in music, and many times (especially in jazz) when melody notes and chord tones don't match. But the concept of using chords that are in a key to accompany a melody based on the notes taken from that key is the backbone of popular music, and if you know the I, IV, and V chords, you can play thousands of songs.

Musicians often talk to each other in numbers. They'll say something like "This song is a I-IV-V in E." So let's see if we can take that piece of information and figure out which chords to play. To find the I, IV, and V chords in E, you can either go to your scales and count up using the whole-step half-step patterns you learned in Chapter 4. (E is the first note in the E scale, F# is the second, G# is the third, A is the fourth, and B is the fifth.) Or you can glance at the Circle of Fifths, which tells you that A is just counterclockwise of E (so it's the IV) and B is just clockwise of E (so it's the V). And that's all there is to it.

And believe it or not, with the Circle of Fifths and what you know about scales and scale degrees, you now have the tools to build the I-IV-V progression starting on any key on the whole piano.

How to Play Progressions

Understanding how chords are related to each other is half the battle—but only half. Playing and practicing chord progressions is the rest. The goal, after all, is playing the piano—not just thinking you know how to!

Inversions

We're going to start by using the inversions we talked about in Chapter 4. Using inversions makes playing a series of chords easier because it reduces the need for big hand movements in the left hand to get from chord to chord. You might have already noticed in "Jingle Bells" that playing a series of chords (say, a C chord, an F chord, and a G chord) in their root positions is not exactly easy. Those moves from C to F and G to C require big jumps, and big jumps are as risky in piano as they are in figure skating. Even worse, it's wasted effort: in piano, the jumps from root position to root position don't even sound all that great.

Practice Makes Perfect

Choose a chord and play it in its inversions. With a C chord, you'd start by playing C-E-G. Then play E-G-C. Then G-C-E. And so on. When you get comfortable playing the inversions going up the keyboard, come back down. Then do this with the other chords in your progression. You should be able to play any chord in any inversion anywhere on the keyboard quickly and confidently. But don't expect to do this all at once! Choose one key at a time, and work on its three primary chords.

Think about a choir. The various voices—sopranos, altos, tenors, basses—don't jump around. Their notes smoothly connect with each other. This smooth movement is called *voice leading*, and it's what we want to sound like when we play chords on a piano. We don't want to sound like we're jumping all over the place with our left hand;

we want to choose notes that connect smoothly. To practice this, we're going to use our I-IV-V progression. Our progression will consist of these three chords played in the following order: I-IV-I-V-I.

 **Universal Language** _____

> **Voice leading** is the process of arrangement the notes in each chord so that they flow smoothly from one to the next.

To play our progression, we're going to stay in one place as much as possible. Start with the C chord in root position (C-E-G; the C is on the bottom). Now, while holding those C notes, think about the notes in an F chord (F-A-C). The goal is to find the F chord notes that are closest to the notes you are already playing. The C is easy: you're already playing a C, so you keep that note. There's an F that is smack between the E and the G you're already playing; that's about as close as you can get! And there's an A just above the G. Now go back and forth between these two chords. After a while, you should be able to do this with your eyes closed.

Now let's move on to the G chord (the V chord). Again, start with your C chord (C-E-G). The notes in a G chord are G-B-D. We already have the G. You'll want to play the D that is between the C and the E, and the B that is just below the C.

In Figure 5.2, the notes in the C chord are noted in the upper circles (C-E-G). The notes in the F chord are noted in the middle circles (C-F-A). The notes in the G chord are noted in the lower circles (B-D-G). Notice how close together these chords are: It only takes a little finger movement to play all these notes!

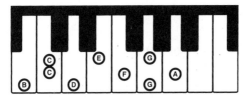

Figure 5.2 *Movement from C to F to G chords.*

Practice Makes Perfect

Using the notes of the scales, you can improvise melodies with your right hand while you are playing your chord progressions with your left hand. When you are playing your C-progression chords, try to improvise with the notes of the C scale starting on C and going up to G (C-D-E-F-G). You may hit a clunker once in a while, but the overall effect should be pleasing.

Using Progressions to Play Songs

Now that you have the chords, it's time to put them to the test—and that means checking out a fake book. You can buy fake books at any music store. Start by choosing a song. Unless you're finding out that you're a total whiz at music theory, you're probably going to want to start with something simple, and that usually means the key of C.

Choosing a Fake Book

There are several perfectly good fake books available that have songs only in the key of C! That's right: the editors have done the hard work for you of transposing (that means moving) the song into the key of C so you can play it using the chords you know. You're looking for three-chord songs. In the key of C, those chords would be C, F, and G. In the next two chapters, you're going to learn so many new chords that you can play any song in any fake book anywhere, but for now, we're sticking with the basics: three chords in a simple key.

Don't confuse a C fake book with a fake book for C instruments. A C fake book simply means that all the songs are written in the key of C, and none of them have any sharps or flats. A fake book for C instruments is edited for a group of instruments—including piano, violins, guitars, flutes, and many others—but the songs themselves can be in any key at all, not just C. Being a C instrument means that when you read a C note and press a C note, you get a C sound. Believe it or not, some instruments do not work this way. With a trumpet, for instance (which is called a B♭ instrument), you read a note that looks like C, and you make that note using the fingering trumpeters call C—but the sound comes out as B♭! The reason has to do with how the instrument is constructed, and it is nothing pianists need to worry about—except to avoid fake books specifically written for these other instruments. (It'll say on the cover "For B♭ instruments," or whatever.)

Playing the Song

To play the song, you need to do two separate jobs. The first is to learn the melody with your right hand. This usually involves playing it several times (and sometimes more). Hum along, and be sure the rhythm is solid. Then practice moving between the chords.

When you put your hands together, you can start by simply playing one chord per measure. Note that after you see a chord symbol, there won't be another chord symbol until the chord changes, even if that is several measures away. You continue to play the same chord (in rhythm) until the change. After you are secure playing the melody with one chord per measure, you might try varying the rhythm a bit. We talk about left-hand rhythmic patterns in Chapter 8.

Moving On

So you're secure with songs in C. What next? The easiest way to learn new keys is to choose songs in the keys that live next door on the Circle of Fifths. For example, after you master C, you could try playing songs in the next-door keys of G or F. The keys that live next door to each other on the Circle of Fifths share two of the three primary chords. For example, the key of G uses G, C, and D—which only requires you to learn one new chord (the D). So after you are comfortable in a key, moving to the key next door requires learning only one new chord.

To get started in a new key, follow the same steps that you used to become comfortable with the three chords in the key of C:

1. Identify the key you're in by checking the key signature and the last chord in the song.

2. Identify the three primary chords in that key.

3. Learn the notes in each of those three chords. (If you've forgotten how to do that, review Chapter 4.)

4. Practice playing them in various inversions up and down the keyboard. Write down the note names if you need a memory aid.

5. Put together your *cadence* by starting with the I chord in root position, and then looking for the nearest notes in the other two chords. Practice your cadence until it feels comfortable.

Universal Language

> A **cadence** is a series of chords that usually occurs near the end of a song, or the end of part of a song, giving it a feeling of rest or resolution.

It may be a little intimidating to realize that each of the 12 notes has its own chord, and that each of these can be played in many different ways. If you've flipped through this book, you've probably noticed that there are still more kinds of chords to learn. And all this while your fingers are still getting used to pushing down three notes at a time and making sure they are the right ones.

Whoa there! Slow down. Rome wasn't built in a day. Pianists don't learn chords as though they were memorizing long lists of vocabulary words the night before the SATs. Quite the opposite. The best way to learn chords is one at a time—at your own pace, as and when you need them.

You'll also find that as you learn more and more chords, the learning gets easier and easier. That's because each of these chords and cadences uses the same patterns of steps and half steps. By the time you get to the "hard" keys, you're going to be wondering what all the fuss was about!

Learn the primary cadence (I-IV-V chords) in one key at a time. Then try your hand at a few songs in that key, looking for songs that only contain the three primary chords. After you're comfortable with that key, you're ready to try another.

The Least You Need to Know

- The Circle of Fifths tells you which chords are related to which other chords.
- Each key has three primary chords, which are next door on the Circle of Fifths.
- The I-IV-V chord progression is the most common progression in popular music (and much classical music, too).
- Playing cadences using inversions is easier than playing in root position and sounds better.
- Start by choosing songs in the key of C that use only three chords.

Chapter 6

More Triads: The Rest of the Gang

In This Chapter

- Understanding how chords are named and numbered
- Building minor, diminished, augmented, and suspended chords
- Using the Circle of Fifths with minor chords and keys
- Playing songs from a fake book using the chords you know

By this point in your piano explorations, you've probably gotten pretty good at building your basic major triad, and you've used it in combination with other major triads in the I-IV-V progression. Now it's time to look at the other types of three-note chords you'll encounter as you make your way through a fake book.

There's good news and good news. First, the chords you'll learn in this chapter have interesting sound characters. Using what we already know about scales and the Circle of Fifths, we'll talk about minor chords and minor keys, as well as other chords that give a sophisticated edge to your playing.

The other good news is that now that you've mastered your basic triads, these new chords are a cinch to learn. To build them, you merely make simple and predictable alterations to the chords you already know. Finally, you'll learn that if you can build your basic major triad and the chords in this chapter, you can play at least a simplified version of virtually any song in any key in any fake book—even jazz!

Scales and the Chords That Go with Them

You already know that we can build chords starting on any note (or degree) of any scale. In any major scale—no matter what note it starts on—the chords built on the first, fourth, and fifth degrees are major. These are the I, IV, and V chords we discussed in Chapter 5. The chords built on the second, third, and sixth degrees are minor. Minor chords, which we discuss in a moment, are noted by small Roman letters (ii, iii, and vi, for example).

Music to Your Ears

You can think of a scale as a collection of notes that sound good together. In western music, we use major and minor scales as the foundation of our tunes, but musicians use many other scales, some dating from the Middle Ages. Readily identifiable sounds such as blues, Middle Eastern music, Chinese music, and traditional church chants are all based on different types of scales.

Minor Chords

Minor chords have a very different sound than their major counterparts. You'll hear the difference the minute you play one. The major chord has what many people describe as a happy sound, whereas the minor chord is something you might choose if you were writing in a more somber mood.

Making a Minor Chord

There are actually three ways to make a minor chord. The easiest is to make a major chord and move the middle note down by a half a step (see Figure 6.1).

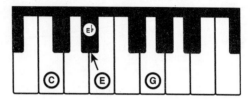

Figure 6.1 *C major becomes C minor when you move the E down a half step to E♭.*

That's all there is to it. Go ahead and try it on the piano so you can hear what this new chord sounds like. Play your C major chord (C-E-G). Then play C minor (C-E♭-G). The difference in sound should be as distinct to you as sunlight and shade. Beethoven used the C minor chord as the foundation for his "Pathetique" sonata, which about sums it up.

You will find minor chords in happy tunes as well as sad tunes. In minor-key tunes, minor chords define the entire character of the piece, whereas in major-key tunes, they add moments of different flavor. Minor chords make an interesting bridge between two major chords and remind us that even on happy days, a cloud might pass.

The second way to build a minor chord is to use the step method (see Figure 6.2) that we used to make major chords in Chapter 4. To make a minor chord starting on any note, count up a step and a half to find the middle note, then go up two full steps to find the top note.

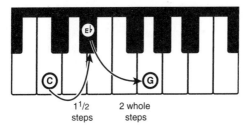

Figure 6.2 *Finding a minor chord using the step method.*

The third way to build a minor chord is to use the minor scale you learned in Chapter 4. Just like when we built a major chord using the scale, you can build a minor chord using the first, third, and fifth notes of the minor scale. You'll find the notes of all the minor scales in Appendix C. Professional pianists use all three methods, especially when building the more complex chords you'll learn about in Chapter 9.

Minor Chords and the Circle of Fifths

So which minor chords are you going to have to play right off the bat? You can go back to the Circle of Fifths for the answer to this question.

Notice that in the diagram below, we've added some new information to our Circle of Fifths. Remember that every major key has a relative minor key and that any minor scale has the same number of sharps or flats as its relative major. In this more complete Circle of Fifths, you can see that in addition to the major key (written in capital letters—let's say C) you also have a small letter.

(If the capital letter is C, the small letter is a.) That key that is written in a lowercase letter is the relative minor of the key written in a capital letter.

 Music to Your Ears _____

The convention in noting chords is that major chords and keys are designated by capital letters (A). Sometimes, minor keys and chords are written with lowercase letters. They can also be written with an uppercase letter follow by the symbol m or min (or, sometimes, a minus sign). A small m *always* indicates a minor chord. A capital M does not apply to the basic triad, which is assumed to be major. A capital M means "major," but it is usually applied to additions to the triad—notes that come after the basic chord. We discuss this confusing distinction in Chapter 7. If you are using Roman numerals, major chords are shown in uppercase (IV) and minor chords are shown in lowercase (iv).

To learn which minor chords will be most likely to appear in a song in a major key, go to the pie piece that has the major key signature. In Chapter 5, you went to the pie pieces on either side of the home key and found the most common major chords. To find the minor chords you'll most likely use, all you do is add the minor chords in those pie pieces (see Figure 6.3). If a song in a major key is going to have minor chords, chances are it's going to be one of these.

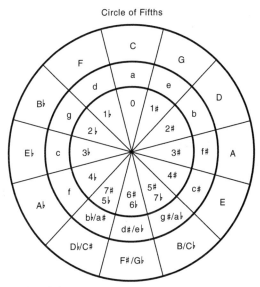

outside circle is major key
middle circle is relative minor key
inner circle is number of sharps or flats

Figure 6.3 *Circle of Fifths with major and minor chords.*

So you know that if you are playing in the key of C, you also know …

1. The three most common major chords you will use are C, F, and G.

2. The three most common minor chords in the key of C are the relative minors of those three major chords.

3. These relative minors are: Am, Dm, and Em.

Songs in Minor Keys

What if your song is in a minor key? Finding the chords for minor keys works the same way. Go to the pie piece that contains the name of the minor key. Just like with the major keys, your most often used chords (both major and minor) will be those in that pie piece and in those immediately clockwise and counterclockwise. So a song in A minor often uses the same chords as a song in C major. This makes sense because they are related keys. You might be wondering, "If they use the same chords, then how come a major key tune and a minor key tune sound so different?" The answer has to do with which chords go where in relation to which other chords—something you don't have to worry about because the composer gives you this information in the lead sheet.

There is one more chord you'll find yourself using a lot when you play a chord in a minor key. This is the major form of the V chord. Yikes! What on earth is *that* supposed to mean? On the Circle of Fifths, it simply means that you start on your home key, let's say A minor. Go one stop clockwise to the slice that says "G major and E minor." You can make the E minor chord an E major chord by raising its middle note one half step.

Music to Your Ears

The Circle of Fifths helps musicians understand how chords are related to each other. In this book, we're using the Circle of Fifths to help us find chords that are often played with other chords, to remember the key signatures (the number of sharps and flats), and to identify major and minor keys that are related. The Circle of Fifths can also be used to analyze the chord progressions of more complicated songs—but that's a topic for another book.

E is the fifth degree of the A minor scale. A song in A minor can use either the E minor chord or the E major chord, depending on the melody notes and the sound the composer wants. In minor keys, the major form of the V chord is very common because it leads nicely back home to the original tonal center. We talk more about this in Chapter 7.

Common Progressions with the Minor Chord

In Chapter 5, you learned the most common chord progression in major keys using major chords. There are a few other chord progressions, either in minor keys or using minor chords, that you will see quite frequently.

It's well worth practicing these chord progressions, because you will encounter them—or fragments of them—in hundreds of songs. Being able to play several chords reliably, one after the other, means that you don't have to worry so much about what you are playing. You can instead concentrate on how you are playing.

Practice these progressions starting in one key. As you did with your I-IV-V progressions, start by identifying (and writing down, if necessary) the notes in all the chords in your progression. Then find the root position of the starting chord, and find the inversions of the other chords that require the least movement of your hand. With the following progressions, we'll use the keys of C major and A minor, because they are related keys that use many of the same chords.

To practice these progressions, simply repeat them over and over. You can use your right hand to play an improvisation based on the C major or A minor scales while your left hand is getting good at the chords.

Major key progressions:

- **ii-V-I.** In the key of C, these chords are Dm-G-C. This is the most common progression in jazz.

- **I-vi-IV-V.** In the key of C, these chords are C-Am-F-G. This is the progression to the favorite children's piano duet of all time: "Heart and Soul." It's also the progression to "Last Kiss" (famously recorded by Pearl Jam) and "Stand By Me" (by Ben E. King;

John Lennon recorded it, too). A variation is I-vi-ii-V. In the key of C, instead of playing F as the third chord, you play the closely related D minor. In addition to songs that stick with that progression the whole way through, thousands use it as part of a verse or chorus.

Minor key progressions:

- **ii-V-i.** In the key of A minor, this progression is Bdim-E-Am. (We discuss the "dim" or diminished chord below; Bdim contains the notes B, D, and F.) This is one of the most common minor-key progressions in jazz. In jazz, however, other notes are frequently added (see Chapters 7 and 9).

- **i-VII-VI-V.** This is the progression to "Greensleeves." Many other songs simply use i-VII-VI. In the key of A minor, the chords are Am-G-F. This is an easy one to play because you can play each chord in its root position.

Other Triads

In addition to the minor triad, you'll need to know several other triads, each of which has a slightly different sound.

The Diminished Chord

Diminished chords aren't quite as common as minor chords, but they are used a lot to move from one chord to another, especially in jazzier tunes. Using chords such as the diminished chord and the augmented chord, which we talk about below, is one of the ways that composers move songs from the simplicity of, say, a children's nursery song to a complex jazz tune.

A diminished chord is notated as °. To make a diminished chord, start with the minor chord and lower the top note one half step (see Figure 6.4).

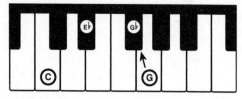

Figure 6.4 *Making a diminished chord.*

You could also use the step method by starting on the root, going up a step and a half step (*a minor third*), and then going up another step and a half (another minor third). Because you are going up the same number of steps each time, it's easy to remember how to build a diminished chord using the step method.

Universal Language

A **major third** is a distance of two whole steps. It is, for instance, the distance from C to E. A **minor third** is a distance of one and a half steps. It is the distance from C to E♭. Major and minor thirds are frequently used to describe the distance between notes in a chord.

Augmented Chords

Augmented chords are also used to give an added edge to a song. Although they aren't the most common chords in your fake book, you will find them in popular songs, jazz songs, and even hymns. An augmented chord uses a raised, or augmented, fifth, and is notated as + or aug (see Figure 6.5).

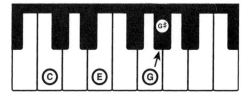

Figure 6.5 *To build an augmented chord, you start with a major chord and raise the top note (the fifth) of the chord by one half step.*

Using the step method, you start on the root, then go up two steps (a *major third*). From there, you go up another two steps (another major third). Like the diminished chord, augmented chords are easy to build because they consist of two intervals that are exactly the same. Therefore, many pianists make this chord using the step method.

Suspended Chords

Another symbol you'll sometimes see is sus, which is short for the word *suspended*, sometimes followed by a number. And indeed, a sus chord has a sort of unstable, "I'm not where I'm supposed to be" sound. The sus chord is used a lot in popular music and rock 'n' roll, but those guys didn't invent it: you'll find it in Beethoven and Bach, too.

In a sus chord, the first thing you do is get rid of the middle note of the triad. You replace it with either the second note in your five-note scale (making the chord a sus 2) or the fourth note of your five-note scale (making the chord a sus 4). A sus 4 is more common than a sus 2. If the instructions merely say sus, you can assume they want you to play a sus 4 chord.

Practice going back and forth between a sus chord and a major chord. You can play around with sus chords, even if they're not written into the music. Sometimes they'll sound good and interesting and they'll liven things up, and sometimes they won't. You'll never know unless you try.

Don't bother to try to find the sus chord using the interval method: it's much easier just to move the third around. Because the sus chord is often played in conjunction with the basic triad, most players find it much easier to think of this chord in relation to the basic major triad.

Practice Makes Perfect

Is chord confusion setting in? Spend a few minutes of each practice session quizzing yourself with a set of homemade flashcards. On each card, write the name of a different chord. (You should have five chords for each key: major, minor, augmented, diminished, and suspended). Grab a card and play the chord in different inversions up and down the keyboard.

Power Chords

A power chord is technically not a chord at all. It's just two notes: the first note of the scale and the fifth note of the scale. This chord is neither major nor minor. Power chords are used mostly by guitarists, who like to distort them with their amplifiers and effects pedals. It's unusual for a power chord to be noted in keyboard music, but if you see C5 (or A5, or any other note followed by a 5), you've got one. To play power chords (and to stay out of the way of a guitar player on a power-chord trip), just play the first note of your five-note scale and the fifth note of your five-note scale.

Taking Stock

Congratulations! You know now how to build every basic triad you will see in a fake book. That's it. There ain't no more.

Does that mean you can really play any song you like? Yes, with some caveats. As you leaf through a fake book, you'll notice that in addition to the basic triad, you may see some other symbols. What, for instance, would you make of a B♭ ♭9#11?

Well, don't run in the other direction just yet, because as with so much of making music, this is yet one more example of the bark being worse than the bite. The complicated-looking B♭ ♭9#11 chord is really made up of two parts, and you already have the most important part—the first part—down cold.

Complex chords are divided into the basic triad (that's the B♭ in this case) and the extra notes (which is what all that ♭9#11 stuff is about). We cover these extra notes in Chapters 7 and 9. For now, feel free to simply ignore part two. Go ahead and wander through any fake book you like. If you encounter a growling monster in the form of a ♭13 or a M9, just play the triad and forget the rest. The more comfortable you are with your basic triads, the easier it's going to be to fancy them up later on. So go have fun: nothing is off limits.

If you're not yet comfortable with diminished or augmented chords, and you think the song is going to sound demented if you even try them, skip that song and pick one that contains the basic major and minor triads. (This will be easy; thousands upon thousands of popular songs don't have diminished, suspended, or augmented chords.) But be sure you play the correct triad: playing a major chord when the song asks for an augmented, or a minor chord when the songs demands a diminished, can lead to noisy clashes between your left hand and your right hand.

Music to Your Ears

Many people think of chord sheets as a modern method of playing, but the practice of writing out accompaniments with chords and symbols is actually several hundred years old. In the Baroque era of the early 1700s, performers were expected to improvise—just like jazz and pop musicians today—and they used chord symbols that are remarkably similar to what we use today.

The Least You Need to Know

- Triads can be changed and manipulated to make different-sounding chords.
- To make a minor chord, lower the middle note.

- Several common chord progressions that use minor chords appear in thousands of songs.

- Augmented, diminished, and suspended chords can be built by making small alterations to major and minor triads.

- When you know how to build all your triads, you have the knowledge to play a basic arrangement of any song in any fake book.

Chapter 7

Four-Note Chords

In This Chapter

- Building and using the dominant seventh chord
- Building major, minor, and diminished seventh chords
- Playing progressions with seventh chords
- Building sixth chords

If you've tried your hand at some songs in a fake book, you've probably noticed two things. First, the basic triads you already know are enough to let you play a serviceable arrangement of just about any song you choose. But second, when you leave off the parts of the chords you don't yet know—the sevenths and sixths and other additions to the basic three-note chords—your song sounds a little empty.

Think of your song as a holiday meal. The triads you already know are the basic ingredients—the meat, the vegetables, and so on. But every good holiday meal also has trimmings and spices—those are your extra notes. Some trimmings and spices are more important than others. You might not mind if Aunt Suzie leaves home the JELL-O and fruit desert, but you sure don't want to miss the gravy and cranberry sauce.

In this chapter, we look at some chords that fall into the "gravy and the cranberry sauce" category. But remember: you do have a safety net. You don't absolutely have to play these extra notes. When the song is moving too fast and the chords get confusing, remember that you can always fall back on the basic triads you've learned so far.

Flavors of Sevenths

By far the most common note to add to a triad is a seventh. But sevenths come in several flavors, so let's start by getting our lingo straight.

The major seventh refers to the seventh degree of the major scale. A C major seventh chord is usually indicated as CM7 and includes the notes of the C major triad (indicated by the C part of the chord) plus B (the seventh note of the C major scale). The letter M in the chord symbol applies to the seventh, not the triad itself. You can also think of a major seventh as being one half step below the note that is the name of the chord.

The flatted seventh is one full step below the name of the chord. This chord symbol has two parts: the type of triad (and it can be any type of triad) and a numeral seven. A C major triad with a flatted seventh is written C7. The C tells you it's a major triad; the 7 tells you it has a flatted seventh added to it. A C minor triad with a flatted seventh is written Cm7. Notice the lowercase m in the C minor 7 chord. The small letter m always refers to the triad, never to the seventh.

The diminished seventh is one and a half steps below the name of the chord (or one half step below the flatted seventh). It is written Cdim7 or C°7. If you're really up on your music theory, you might protest, "Hey, but isn't that a sixth, not a seventh?" Well, er, yes, but we call it a diminished seventh anyway.

 Sour Notes _____

> Sevenths can be confusing at first. After you've learned the different types of sevenths, practice playing and listening to them so you get their sounds in your ear. The different kinds of sevenths are not interchangeable with each other. When in doubt, it's better to drop the seventh entirely than play the wrong one.

We discuss all of these chords in detail in the sections that follow.

The Dominant Seventh

The dominant seventh is a type of flatted seventh chord, and as the most common, flexible, and important seventh chord, it deserves first billing (see Figure 7.1). This chord is built with a major triad and a flatted seventh added to it (for instance, G7). It is considered a dominant seventh chord if it is built on the fifth degree of the key you're playing in. (For example, in the key of C, the dominant seventh is the G7 chord.) This chord is so common that you'll see it in virtually every song in virtually every fake book—as well as in almost everything ever written by a classical composer. Of all the chords in this chapter, the dominant seventh chord is the easiest to learn, and the most important to know.

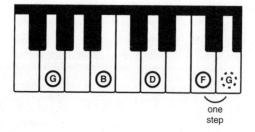

Figure 7.1 *The G7 chord. Note that the added note, F, is one full step below G. You do not have to play the second G; it's just here for illustration.*

What the Dominant Seventh Does

The dominant seventh chord is used in a variety of ways. If your song has a big climactic ending, chances are that a dominant seventh chord is the second-to-last chord. The dominant seventh chord is the chord that tells you "It's time to end the song now." It leads back to the home chord, and when you hit the ending, the audience knows they can start to clap and go home. The dominant seventh is also used in the middle of the song, often to help change key temporarily, or to help the song come to a moment of rest or stability before moving on.

Go ahead and play your G7 chord (G-B-D-F) on the piano. It sounds like it's unstable, doesn't it? Not only that: if you heard it at the end of a song, you would know that the song wasn't quite finished. Your inner ear probably already knows what that next, final chord has to be. Play the G7 chord again, then follow it with a big crashing C chord (C-E-G). That's a familiar sound, isn't it? The dominant seventh chord (in this case, G7) leads you home (in this case to C).

Simplifying the Seventh Chord

I can almost hear you muttering: "I'm supposed to play with four fingers at once? Not a chance."

Well, relax, because there are easier ways to play the dominant seventh chord. You're allowed to leave some notes out. In fact, sometimes it even sounds better.

Music to Your Ears _____

The dominant seventh chord has such a strong pull toward the tonic that composers often use it in minor keys, too, even though—if you want to get technical about it—one of the notes in the dominant seventh chord doesn't belong to the key. Take A minor (which has no sharps or flats): the fifth degree of this scale is E, so the dominant seventh chord is E7 (E-G#-B-D). But G# is not in the A minor scale. To avoid too much dissonance and to match the dominant seventh chord, you will frequently see a raised seventh in the melody. In the key of A minor, this means that instead of (or sometimes in addition to) the G, which is the normal (natural) seventh degree of the A minor scale, you might find a G# in the melody to match the G# in the E7 chord.

The easiest way to simplify a dominant seventh chord is to play just two notes: the note that the chord is named after and the seventh (the note that is a full step below the name of the chord). So in this case, instead of playing all four notes of a G7 chord, you can simply play a G and an F.

Try it: with your left hand, go ahead and play a G with your thumb, and put the second finger on F.

Play this two-note chord, then follow it with your basic C major chord in root position. Sounds pretty good, doesn't it?

Another way to simplify the dominant seventh chord is to play three of its notes. But which three? Start by keeping the notes in the simplified two-note version we just talked about.

The two notes that are left are the third (in this case, a B) and the fifth (in this case, a D). Of those two notes, most pianists choose to keep the third (the middle note of the basic triad). The reason is that the third is the note that determines whether the character of the chord is major or minor. The fifth, as it turns out, is the most dispensable, so we leave out the D (see Figure 7.2). Our three-note G7 chord is now G-B-F. To play the chord in root position with your left hand, you play the G with your pinky, the B with your ring finger, and the F with your thumb.

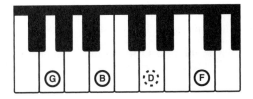

Figure 7.2   *Three-note version of a G7 chord in root position. The D is dropped.*

Here's even better news—not only does dropping the top note of the triad (also called the fifth) make playing easier, in many cases it actually sounds better because you don't have so many growling notes clamoring for attention down in the bass. Dropping the fifth opens things up a bit, letting the chord breathe, so to speak.

Inversions: More Easy Tricks

Another way to make your life at the piano easier is to remember that there's no rule that says you have to play the notes of a chord in any particular order. We explored inversions in Chapter 5. We can invert seventh chords, too.

Let's say you are playing a C chord, and you want to move to a G7 chord and then back to a C chord. Begin with the C chord in its usual root position (C-E-G). Go ahead and play it with your left hand. Your pinky is on C, finger 3 is on E, and your thumb is on G. Now, you want to move to a G7 chord. But moving from a C chord in root position (C on the bottom) to a G7 chord in root position (G on the bottom) is a lot of work. You've got to pick up your hand, move it up five notes, and then find all the notes in the G7 chord.

There is a much easier way—and it sounds better, too (see Figure 7.3). Go back to the C chord. Play it and hold your fingers down. This time, instead of jumping all the way up to G to play the G7 chord, you're going to look for the notes in the G7 chord that are closest to the C-chord notes you are already holding down. Remember that your three-note G7 chord contains G, B, and F.

Well, the G is a no-brainer—we already have our thumb sitting right on it. The F is almost as easy: There's an F just one note down from G, so our second finger will play that. As it turns out, this is just our simplified two-note version of the chord. If you want, you can stop right here.

If you want the fuller sound of the three-note G7 chord, you need to add the B. The nearest B is the one that is right below the C, so stretch your pinky and put it there. Let's leave out the D for now; it's completely optional.

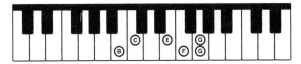

Figure 7.3 *The C notes of the C chords are in the upper circles; the notes of the three-note G7 chord are in the lower circles.*

Practice Makes Perfect

Try going back and forth between the C chord and the G7 chord until you get comfortable. You'll be seeing a lot of this progression, so get comfortable with it. Then try finding the dominant seventh chord in other keys. Practicing going back and forth between all the V7 and I chords is probably the most effective two-chord practice exercise you can do, because you will see this progression in virtually every song you play.

It's All About Patterns

It might have occurred to you as you were practicing your C-G7-C progression that there are 11 more keys. And yes, to play in all of them, you have to practice your progressions starting on any note.

But let me set your mind at rest. First of all, you don't have to learn all 12 keys today. In fact, you might spend your entire piano-playing career and never even play a song in F sharp! To start, stay with songs in the simpler keys (C and its closest neighbors on the Circle of Fifths).

Music to Your Ears

Not every pianist uses inversions, and some beginners find them difficult to master, especially at full tempo. If you are more comfortable playing your chords in root position, there's no reason why you can't stay there for a while—if fact, some songs sound nice that way. So feel free to use root-position chords if that's easier for you, and work in an inversion or two as you get comfortable with them.

Second, you already know most of what you need to know to play these I-V7-I progressions in other keys. The pattern you learned for the G7-C progression works on any key. Not only that, most people find that after they have mastered the chords in two or three keys, the rest just seem to fall into place.

Here are some rules to get you started.

To play a I-V7-I progression starting on any key using a simplified 2-note V7 chord ...

- Play the I chord. (That's the starting and ending chord.)
- To play the V7 chord, simply play the top note (the fifth) of the I chord and the note that is one full step beneath it.
- Go back to the I chord.

To play a I-V7-I progression starting on any key using a three-note V7 chord ...

- Play the I chord.
- Find the two-note version of the V7 chord (as previously described).
- Add the note that is one half step below the first note (the root) of the I chord. This gives you a three-note V7 chord.
- Go back to the I chord.

At Sixes and Sevens

You will encounter several other four-note chords. As with all other chords containing more than three notes, the extra notes are optional—but if you want to develop interesting arrangements, you are going to want to explore these new sounds as soon as your basic triads are secure.

The Minor Seventh Chord

When a flatted seventh is added to a minor triad, you get a minor seventh chord. The effect isn't as strong, but minor sevenths are common chords, especially in minor-key songs and in jazz. The formula is exactly the same as it is for a dominant seventh chord: starting with the basic triad, you add the note that is a full step below the chord's name. You can also think of the seventh as the note that is a step and a half above the highest note in the basic triad.

Let's compare the notes in a dominant seventh and a minor seventh in Figure 7.4.

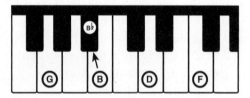

Figure 7.4 *A G7 chord becomes a Gm7 chord by lowering the B by one half step.*

The G7 chord you learned earlier contains G-B-D-F. The Gm7 chord contains G-B♭-D-F. Play the dominant seventh and the minor seventh back to back a few times to see how they compare.

The Major Seventh

The major seventh chord sounds completely different than the dominant seventh, and is never inter-
changeable with it. It is a common jazz chord. To
many beginning pianists, it sounds a bit dissonant.

To make a major seventh, start with a major triad
and add the note that is one half step below the
name of the chord (see Figure 7.5). (This will be
the seventh note of the major scale.) This chord
might sound harsh at first, but give it time; it's a
sound that grows on you.

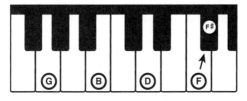

Figure 7.5   *A G7 chord becomes a GM7 by raising the highest
note (the "seventh") by one half step.*

In addition to jazz, you'll find this chord in the
music of Bach, Chopin, and many other classical
composers. A major seventh is most commonly
added to a major triad. It can be also added to a
minor triad (in which case you'd have a chord
notated as GmM7). But this is less common.

♪ 🎵 **Sour Notes**

> The scale method of building chords can be confusing when you're talking about sevenths. That's because the type of seventh you use and the scale it comes from don't always match up as you might expect. You can safely use the scale method to build the major seventh chord (add the seventh degree of the scale to your major triad). But the seventh you use in the dominant chord belongs to a different scale: it is flatted, or one half step below, the major seventh. Just remember that if you hear the word *seventh*, it always means a flatted seventh—one full step below the name of the chord.

Diminished Sevenths

Remember how we built our diminished triad in Chapter 6? Like every other chord, a diminished chord starts on the note it is named after. To build the triad, you add the note that is a step and a half up from your starting note. Then you add a third note, which is also a step and a half up from your second note. To make a fully diminished seventh chord, you go up another step and a half, as shown in Figure 7.6.

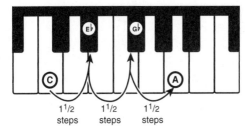

Figure 7.6   *Cdim 7.*

Augmented, Suspended, Demented

Okay, there's no such thing as a demented chord. (You may disagree.) But any triad—major, minor, augmented, diminished, suspended, and anything else you can dream up—can have a seventh added to it. Most often, the seventh you are adding is the flatted seventh—the seventh that is one full step down from the note name.

If you add a seventh to a diminished chord, you get what is called a "half-diminished seventh," also called a "minor seven flat five." Don't sweat these scary-sounding names: just take them one piece of information at a time (see Figure 7.7). There is method to the madness: Calling this chord a half-diminished seventh distinguishes it from the fully diminished seventh chord just described. Calling it a minor seven flat five is cumbersome but infor-mative: it tells you that it's a minor chord, with a flatted seventh, and that the fifth is flatted, or diminished. This chord is most commonly used in minor-key jazz tunes, especially in ii-V-I progres-sions, which, now that you are learning more chords, can be played as iim7b5-V7-i.

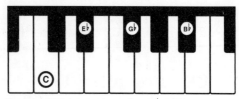

Figure 7.7 *C°7 (also written Cmin7♭5: C minor seven flat five). The E♭ makes it minor. The G♭ makes the five flat. And the B♭ is the seventh.*

You can add a seventh to a suspended chord: just play the suspended triad and add the flatted seventh. If it's a C chord, it is notated C7sus4 or Csus7, and contains C-F-G-B♭.

Music to Your Ears _____

As you start to play more advanced chords, you will notice that some chords of the different names contain the exact same notes. For example, a C6 chord consists of C-E-G-A—and an Am7 chord consists of an A-C-E-G—same notes, different order. Don't worry about this: all you have to do is find the right notes. There are two reasons for the different names. First, there are conventions in music theory having to do with certain chords following certain other chords. And second, the way the chord is named gives you clues about what other notes can be added to it (we talk about this in Chapter 9) and which notes you can safely improvise with.

You can also add a seventh to an augmented chord: just play the augmented triad and add the flatted seventh. A C augmented 7 chord is written Caug7 and contains C-E-G#-B♭.

Sixths

Sixths have the same floating intriguing character as major seventh chords, but to many people they sound slightly less dissonant. They can often be substituted for a major seventh chord, or a sixth can be added to a major seventh chord, especially as a passing tone. To play a sixth chord, you add the note that is one full step above the fifth (see Figure 7.8).

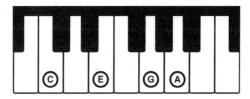

Figure 7.8 *C6. Add the note (in this case A) that is one full step above the top note in the triad (in this case G).*

It doesn't matter whether the starting triad is major or minor: the sixth is always one full step above the fifth.

The Least You Need to Know

- Sevenths are the most common additions to triads.

- Major sevenths are made by adding the note that is one half step below the name of the chord.

- To make a dominant seventh chord, start with a major triad and add the flatted seventh, which is the note that is one full step below the name of the chord.

- The flatted seventh can also be added to all the other triads.

- The sixth (the note that is one full step above the top note of a triad) can be added to major and minor triads.

Chapter 8

Putting It All Together

In This Chapter

- Voicing chords so they sound good
- Creating chord patterns for your right and left hands
- Playing the blues
- Using slash chords, passing tones, and other tricks of the trade

Now that you know all these chords, it's time to start being creative with them. You have the tools to move beyond simplified fake books and simple three-chord songs to a wide variety of songs in different styles. You also have the tools to take a simple song and make it more interesting.

Being able to play your chords and chord progressions confidently is the first and most important part of the equation. The next part is the fun part: figuring out how to turn a series of chords into a complete accompaniment.

This is where you start to experiment. In this chapter, we cover the basics of left-hand chord patterns and accompaniment tricks.

Voicings

Some of the chords you learned in Chapter 7 might sound a little new to you. The major seventh chord is one that many pianists find a little dissonant at first. Diminished and augmented chords may also be sounds you're not familiar with yet. In Chapter 9, we look at a few chords that may sound even more dissonant to you. However, don't reject these chords before you've given them a full hearing. Dissonance adds interesting spice and tension to a song if it's used tastefully, and there are many ways to control the dissonance of any given chord. Remember that you can play the notes of any chord in any order, anywhere on the keyboard. This is important because combinations of notes sound better in some places than in others.

 Sour Notes

Great musicians will often tell you that the notes they leave out are as important as the notes they leave in. Don't feel you have to play every note in every chord all the time—breaking them up, leaving notes out, and carefully choosing which notes to emphasize all make you a more subtle, interesting pianist. Too many notes can do exactly the opposite!

So far, we've used progressions relying on close voicings, which means that the notes of a chord are played within the same octave. But as you learned in Chapter 4, no rule says you have to play all the notes of a chord so close together—you can play them all over the piano, wherever they sound good. Here are some voicing techniques to try:

- **Open voicing.** Spread out the notes! You can play the 1 and the 5 in the left hand and the 3 and the 7 in the right hand.

- **Rootless voicing.** This is more common when you are playing with a bass player. The bass player's territory is the bottom couple of octaves of the piano. A good pianist stays out of the bass player's way, which means not playing chord roots down low.

- **Partial chords.** You don't always have to play every note of a chord. For a light, airy feeling, just two notes often do nicely, especially when the changes are very fast.

- **Don't clutter the bass!** After you drop five or six notes below middle C, you're in the range of the piano where too many notes played together can sound muddy.

- **Break up the chord with a rhythmic pattern.** You could play the lowest note of the chord alone, and then follow with the rest of the chord, so as to divide the chord between two beats.

Putting a Song Together

Learning a song via the chord method is a fairly straightforward process. First, you learn the melody. Even if you are a band keyboardist who never touches the melody, you should still know the tune. The subtleties of the melody will inform your chord and voicing choices, your passing tones, and your improvisational ideas. Plus you need to know where you come in, and to know that, you need to know how the song goes. So play the tune through a few times.

Then it's time for the chords. Start by playing the chords alone. You can start with all the chords in root position, if that's most comfortable for you. More advanced pianists will use inversions and voicings they've come to know; but if you're still looking for the notes in any given chord, root position is a better place to start. Play one chord per beat. Sometimes you'll be able to play one chord for an entire measure. Other times, you'll have to change chords in the middle of a measure. Or you may have to play three or even four chords in a single measure. Play the changes on the beat that is indicated, and practice playing the chords in rhythm.

After you have the chords in your ear and you've reviewed the notes in each of them, experiment with different inversions and voicings. Keep an eye out for the common patterns you've learned and practiced: IV-V-I, ii-V-I, I-vi-IV-V, or some of the other common progressions we've covered. Choose voicings you know using the inversions you've practiced, or new voicings that require a minimum amount of hand movement.

What you do next very much depends on whether you will be playing solo or with a band. If you're the soloist, then your right hand is going to be responsible for the melody (although it can help out with harmony, too, as we discuss in a minute). Your left hand has the job of keeping a steady beat and playing the chords in a way that supports the melody. If you're playing with a band, both hands can share chord-playing duties—which gives you a lot of flexibility.

In either case, you're going to want to do more than just play the chords over and over, one to a beat.

Left-Hand Patterns

The number of left-hand patterns you can come up with is limited only by your creativity. Figures 8.1 through 8.5 are some examples of how the notes in a basic major triad can be broken up and rearranged in repeated patterns that give body to the harmony.

Figure 8.1 *In the first measure, we break the chord into two and play the root, followed by the rest of the chord on the second beat. Then we repeat the two-beat pattern. In the second pattern, we play the root, the rest of the chord, then the fifth and the top notes of the chord.*

Figure 8.2 *The waltz pattern is the most common pattern in three quarter time. Like the previous pattern, it involves breaking up the chord into its root followed by the rest of the chord played twice in a row.*

Figure 8.3 *This classical pattern works with slower balladlike songs. You can vary it in different ways: 1) Lower note–upper note–middle note–upper note. 2) Lower note–middle note–upper note– middle note.*

Figure 8.4 *In an arpeggio, notes of a chord are played one at a time in order from bottom to top and (if you like) back down again. Arpeggios can be short, as in this example. More advanced pianists practice them up and down the entire keyboard for a dramatic effect.*

Figure 8.5 *In the first measure, the chord is played only on the off beats (beats 2 and 4, rather than 1 and 3). In the second measure, steady rhythmic riff is repeated in each measure.*

Putting Your Right Hand to Work

For most of this book, we've concentrated on using the left hand to play chords. I've given left-hand fingerings for the chords and left-hand exercises because at the start, your right hand plays the melody and your left hand plays the chords.

But your right hand isn't limited to just the notes in the melody. Indeed, if you're playing in a band, your right hand doesn't play the melody, so it has every bit as much chord playing responsibility as your left hand. And even if you are playing solo, your right hand can help create a fuller sound by adding chord notes and *passing tones*—notes that aren't in the tune or in the chord, but provide nice filler in between.

The trick to using your right hand is to play most of the melody with the third, fourth, and fifth fingers, leaving the second finger and the thumb free to play *chordal tones* and passing tones.

 Universal Language

> **Chordal tones** are notes that are part of the chord you are playing. **Passing tones** are notes that are not part of the chord.

Blues

One of the most common progressions in music is the 12-bar blues. With only a few tweaks, the blues is based on the same I-IV-V progression that you learned in Chapter 5. The only difference is that we add a flatted seventh (dominant seventh) to the three primary chords.

Learning the basic blues progressions is probably the biggest bang you can get for your chord-playing buck. You'll find blues progressions and licks in songs ranging from the Doors ("Riders on the Storm") to Chuck Berry ("Roll Over Beethoven") to the Beach Boys ("Barbara Ann") to Johnny Cash ("Folsum Prison Blues"), not to mention the classic blues of Muddy Waters, B. B. King, and Robert Johnson. A tune doesn't have to be a "blues" song to use elements of the blues. You'll find blues notes and chords in rock 'n' roll, country, and jazz as well as straight blues—which is why this form is so important to know.

The 12-Bar Blues

The 12-bar blues takes its name from the fact that each verse has—you guessed it!—12 bars in it. And these 12 bars repeat over and over, using the same chords in the same order. (There are, of course, variations. Some great players have managed to play songs that break every rule—and still sound like the blues.)

To start, you can think of a blues tune as having three parts, each of which is four measures long. The first two lines use basically the same or similar melodic material, even though the chords change. The last line sums it all up and either turns the song around to go back to the beginning, or ends it. Here's how it works:

1. The first line has four measures, and you play the I7 chord in each measure. In the key of C, that is C7.

2. The second line has four measures. In the first two measures, you play the IV7 chord. In the second two measures, you go back to the I7 chord. Still in the key of C, those are F7 and C7.

3. The third line is the most complicated. In the first measure, you play the V7 chord. In the second measure, you play the IV7 chord. In the third, you play the I7 chord. In the last measure, you have two options. If you are going to go back to the beginning and play another verse, you go to the V7 chord in the last measure. This "turns around" the song and sends you back to the beginning. If you're ending the song, you just stick to the I chord. In C, the chords are G7, F7, and C7, with the turnaround on the G7.

Left-Hand Blues Patterns

Any blues riff book will give you dozens of left-hand patterns, but a common pattern called a blues shuffle can get you started (see Figure 8.6). The pattern involves alternating between the 1 and the 5 and the 1 and the 6 of whatever chord you're playing. Note that the shuffle is first written in a time signature we haven't covered: $\frac{12}{8}$. You can think of this time signature as having four beats to each measure, with each beat divided into three sub-beats. It's also written in swing eighths, which means that they are written as if they were equal-valued eighth notes—but they are played with the first note being longer than the last note. This is extremely common in jazz and blues notation.

Music to Your Ears

Transposing means taking a song that is written in one key and playing it in another. When you transpose, you move everything up or down the exact same number of steps, regardless of black notes or white notes. As with scales, the only thing that counts is the number of steps. This is where thinking in "numbers" helps. If your original song is in C, you can think of the F and G chords as the IV and V chords. To transpose to E, you figure out that the IV and V chords in the key of E are A and B. Use the chart in Appendix C to help you transpose. It lists the chords in each key by degree. All you have to do is figure out the old key and the new key. Then you just go down the columns and substitute the chords in the new key for the chords in the old key.

Figure 8.6   *Blues shuffle written in $\frac{12}{8}$ time and in $\frac{4}{4}$ time with "swing eighths."*

Music to Your Ears

The blues scale is a six-note scale that can be widely used in blues, rock 'n' roll, country music, and many other situations. The blues scales originated in Africa, and the exact pitches are somewhere between the cracks in a piano keyboard. The tension between the blue notes and the major chords is what gives the blues its unique sound.

The six-note blues scale can be understood in relation to the major scale (see Figure 8.7). It contains the 1, the flat 3, the 4, the sharp 4, the 5, and the flat 7. The altered notes (E♭, F#, and B♭) are identified as to how they relate to the major scale. In the key of C, E♭ is the flatted third, F# is the sharp fourth, and B♭ is the flatted seventh. To find the notes in any blues scale, start with the notes of the major scale and make the same alterations.

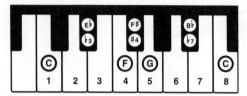

Figure 8.7 *Notes of a C blues scale. The degrees of the C scale are numbered on each note of the C scale. The notes of the blues scale are in circles.*

The notes of a blues scale can also be used as short little grace notes to spice up your chords. For example, instead of playing a simple C chord, you could play your C chord like Figure 8.8.

Figure 8.8 *Using blues notes with chords.*

More Tricks of the Trade

Your left hand isn't limited to chordal tones. It, too, can get creative, especially when moving from one chord to another.

Passing Tones

Using passing tones is a smooth way to connect chords. Because they are not in the chord you are playing, they add a little tension, or dissonance, which can be exciting—or it can simply sound like noise. You need to experiment with how much dissonance you are comfortable with. Passing tones are often used in bass lines and inner voices.

Practice Makes Perfect

Your left hand can do a lot more than play chords, but in order to make the most of passing tones and interesting bass lines, it needs to be agile. Try giving your left hand some extra practice by using it to play the melody. (While you're at it, try playing the chords with your right hand.) The sound of a left-hand melody and a right-hand accompaniment is an interesting twist that works for some songs in performance, as well.

Walking Bass Lines

Walking bass lines are well named (see Figure 8.9). In this technique, the pianist plays a series of notes that step along in strict rhythm form. A very common walking bass line is moving from the I chord to the IV chord, or from the V chord to the I chord. You can play these bass lines going in either direction, up or down the keyboard.

Figure 8.9 *Walking bass line with chords.*

Slash Chords

You may come across a chord symbol that looks like C/B or A7/E. The first letter refers to the chord. The second letter tells which note to play in the bass. The second letter may or may not be a note in the chord itself. The top notes of the chord can be arranged in any order you like. So you could play C/B as B-C-E-G, or you could play it in any other order you choose, as long as the B is on the bottom (for example, B-E-G-C). The presence of slash chords usually indicates that the composer or arranger has a particular bass line in mind, and following these directions often leads to pleasant and interesting voicings of the rest of the chords, as well.

The Least You Need to Know

- Careful voicings, or arrangements of notes in a chord, can help your arrangement sound more interesting, more clear, and more pleasant.

- Chords can be played in blocks, with all the notes played at once, or broken, where the different notes are played at different times.

- The right hand can share chord-playing duties, whether you are playing as a soloist or an ensemble musician.

- The blues is a form that uses a certain predictable sequence of chords and scales, and is used in many types of music.

- Techniques such as passing tones, walking bass lines, and slash chords can enliven a left-hand chord pattern.

9

Advanced Chords: Extensions and Alterations

In This Chapter

- Learning chord extensions and alterations
- Voicing advanced chords
- Experimenting with chord substitutions

Just the name of this chapter is intimidating, isn't it? Not only are we playing chords, we're also playing "advanced" chords. And not only are they advanced, they are extended and altered, too. Whatever that means.

So the first thing we're going to tell you about these chords is: Relax. You don't need them. You may never need them. Read this page, and then skip this entire chapter if you like. You can come back to it later, after you're comfortable playing the chords you've already learned and are interested in something a little funkier, cooler, or more interesting.

The reason we're even dealing with these chords is because—like Mt. Everest—"they're there!" If you pick up any fake book—especially jazz—you'll see them. I don't want you to think you can't play the song. You *can* play the song—in several different ways. One way to handle these chords is to ignore them.

You're allowed to skip the notes that make your head spin. In Chapter 7 you learned that the song isn't going to fall apart if you skip a seventh once in a while (or even more). The same goes for ninths, elevenths, and thirteenths, and other chords we talk about in this chapter. Beyond the basic triad, what you play is optional, especially if you don't care about sounding exactly like the CD. So if you see something like a B♭M9♭13, and you're playing fast and you sure don't know what the flat thirteenth of a B♭ is, just play your B♭ chord. Feel better now?

Chord Extensions

"Okay, but I want it to sound like the CD," you might be saying. Or, "I'm bored; I want to sound more interesting." Or, "Bring 'em on! I'm up for the challenge."

That's when you start using those added notes.

Think of the chord symbol—the sequence of letters, numbers, majors, minors, sharps, and flats—as a recipe that tells you what goes inside. It could be a canned-tomato-soup-add-water-and-stir kind of recipe—say, your C major chord. Or it could be a

Baked-Alaska-freeze-this-bake-that-and-set-the-whole-thing-on-fire sort of recipe—maybe one of those chords with lots of sharps and flats and big numbers added on. But what it comes down to is following a set of directions.

Practice Makes Perfect

Using formulas to make chords is an essential tool, but playing songs will get these more complicated chords into your hands even faster. You'll find these altered and extended chords in many jazz tunes. Most jazz tunes have only one or two difficult chords, making this a pleasant and rewarding way to practice. Once you've learned a difficult chord in one tune, you'll know it the next time you see it in a different tune.

But how do we read the recipe? Yet again, it's all about the scales. The easiest way to handle extended and altered chords is to use what you already know about scales. Let's go back to our old friend the C major scale.

The notes that are usually added to chords are 9s, 11, and 13s. But wait a minute—9s? 11s? 13s? Doesn't the scale only have eight notes? Well, yes—but there's nothing to say you can't keep going (see Figure 9.1).

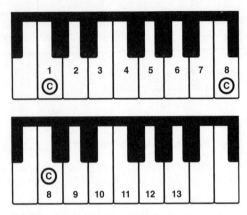

Figure 9.1 *The first keyboard shows the C scale (the top note is middle C, marked in a circle). The second keyboard shows the extended scale from middle C to the C above middle C). In the first octave, the notes are numbered 1–8. The second octave beings with middle C—(numbered 8) and goes up to 13.*

So let's say a chord says C9. You look at the keyboard figure and see that the 9 is a D.

But haven't we already agreed that in the key of C, D is the second degree? What's this 9 business? And what's the difference between a C9 and a Csus2? And isn't there also a chord called the Cadd2? It's enough to make your head spin.

Well, first of all, in the Csus2, we dropped the third. That's what made it a sus chord. In the 9 chord, we're going to keep the third. But what about Cadd2? Doesn't that mean just play a C chord and add a second? It does indeed. Where the 9 chord is different is that it includes a seventh.

In fact, any of these extended chords—chords that use numbers higher than 7—require the presence of a seven. That's what makes them extended. So although 11 can also be thought of as a 4, the 11 chord has to have a 7 in it (and it may have a 9, as well). And a 13—you guessed it—is the same note as the 6, but the 13 chord has to have a 7 (and it may have a 9 and an 11, as well).

There's also a 6-9 chord, which contains the major triad, the 6, and the 9. The 6 and the 9 are often used in conjunction with the major 7, but it is not uncommon to drop the major 7 and just play the 6 and the 9. The 6 can be thought of as a substitute for the major 7. The 6-9 chord is a common jazz chord, especially at the end of a tune.

If you're starting to think this is getting too crowded, you're probably right, which is why musicians rarely play every single possible note in a chord. In Chapter 8, we talked about voicing chords—organizing the notes and spreading them out so they sound good. This becomes crucially important when playing altered and extended chords. Some voicings sound nothing short of horrible, and others—using exactly the same notes, but in different positions—sound ethereal. We talk about some voicing rules a bit later in this chapter.

Altered Chords

The notes added to chords aren't necessarily notes that belong to the scale. The 9, the 11, and the 13 can all be altered (see Figure 9.2). In addition to their normal major forms, the 9 can be either flatted or sharp, the 11 can be sharp, and the 13 can be flatted.

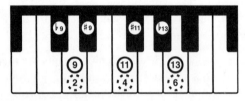

Figure 9.2 *Alterations in the key of C. Note that 9 is the same note as the 2, the 11 is the same note as the 4, and the 13 is the same note as the 6.*

Music to Your Ears _____

Not all alterations will sound good with all chords. How do you know which notes you can add to which chords? Your ear is the first test: if it sounds good, experiment with it. You can also apply alterations that sounded good in one song to a different song and see if they work. If you find yourself intrigued by the possibilities, check out a jazz theory book.

Altered chords are commonly used in jazz tunes. In addition, you might see other symbols in different chord recipes, such as an add4 or a flat 5. All you have to do is follow the instructions. If the symbol says flat 5, lower the fifth by a half step. If it says aug5, raise the fifth. If it says add4, add a fourth.

Voicing Altered and Extended Chords

There are many different schools of thought on voicing chords, and how you voice chords will in part depend on whether you are playing solo or in a group, and—if you are playing in a group—what the other folks are doing. Here are some basic principles that will help you explore what sounds good to you:

- Don't cluster all low tones too close together. This means you have to stretch your left hand and play only a few notes with it. You might play only the 1 and the 7 with the left hand, and let your right hand grab the other notes. A couple of other common left-hand voicings are the 1, the 3, and the 7, the 1 and the 5, or the 1 and the 10 (if you can reach that far).

- Break up the left-hand chord, playing part of it on the first beat, and the rest of it a half beat or a full beat later.

- Try to keep the middle range of the accompaniment—the part that is above the lowest left-hand notes but below the melody—in the region around middle C.

- Control dissonance by spreading out tones that don't sound good together or dropping notes that sound like they clash too much. Often (especially with sharp 11s and flat 13s), this means eliminating the fifth—which, as we already know, is the least necessary note in the basic triad.

- Check to see whether one of the altered or extended notes is also a melody note. If you're playing solo piano, you'll play that note in the melody so you don't need to double it in the harmony. If you're playing in a group, the soloist will get that note. However, if you're playing backup for a shaky singer, ask if she wants you to cue her in on the melody. Sometimes those notes are hard for nonprofessional singers to find.

Adding Notes to Basic Chords

Up to this point, we've been concerned with reading chord symbols as they appear in fake books. But as a pianist, you are not limited to the chords exactly as they are written.

If you are playing from a fake book that has fairly simple chords, you can try adding notes, either as part of the chord itself or as passing tones. This is a bit of a hit-and-miss process: the simpler and more basic the song, the less appropriate a highly complicated dissonant arrangement might be. But then again, that just might be the effect you're looking for. The following suggestions will give your chords a sophisticated jazzy flair:

- With a major triad, try adding a major 7, a 6, or a 9.
- With a minor triad, try adding with a 6, a major 7, or a 9.
- With a minor 7, try adding a 9 or an 11.
- With a dominant seventh, try adding a 9, 11, or 13. This is the most flexible chord of all. Depending on the context of the song and the key and scales it uses, you can also experiment with adding the sharp 11, the augmented 5, and either the flat 9 or the sharp 9.

Music to Your Ears

The examples in this chapter are shown in the key of C major for clarity. Other keys have sharps and flats, which makes it a little trickier at first to figure out the alterations. Remember to think in terms of scale numbers only: it doesn't matter whether the note is black or white. For example, in the key of Ab, the first degree of the scale is Ab, the second degree is Bb, the third degree is C, and the fourth degree (and hence the eleventh degree) is Db. So the sharp 11 would be D natural (One half step higher than the 11, which is Db). Appendix C gives you all the notes and degrees in all the major scales, so you can figure out your alterations from there.

Chord Substitutions

Advanced and confident pianists frequently substitute chords—and indeed, there are whole books written on how to do this! Additionally, in some fake books, you'll see two rows of chord symbols: the standard chords are written in the usual place; the substitute chords will be above them, usually in parentheses or in another color. Try both sets and see which ones you like.

Many music theory rules explain how chord substitutions are arrived at. But that is beyond the scope of this book. What you do need to know is that you are not required to play the chords exactly as written. In fake book playing, you are a co-creator along with the composer. In fact, if you check out five different fake book arrangements of a song, you are likely to see subtle (and sometimes not-so-subtle) differences in the chords used.

So experiment with different alterations and substitutions if you like. Simplify your song—or make it more complex. Just remember that if you do decide to play with others, you need to tell them about any funky chords you've added, or any substitutions you've chosen to use.

The Least You Need to Know

- Extensions and alterations involve adding additional notes to a seventh chord.
- Extensions and alterations require careful voicing to avoid a crowded sound or too much dissonance.

- Chord symbols can be used exactly as written—or you may experiment with substitutions and additions.

Chapter 10

Getting Better: Virtuosos Are Us

In This Chapter

- Learning how to practice
- Playing with recordings
- Playing with others
- Finding a teacher

You now know how to make virtually any chord you'll encounter in any fake book, and the chords you've learned in this book will provide enough material for a lifetime of musical enjoyment. Yet we have only begun to scratch the surface.

So what's next? The chord method doesn't require years of technical exercises and music-reading ability, but it does require practice. It also requires awareness of how you are constructing chords, and which notes you are choosing to put in and leave out.

In this chapter, we look at some of the ways you can improve both your piano thinking and your piano playing—and have fun at the same time.

The Way to Carnegie Hall

Well, you already know the tired old joke. It's been repeated a million times not because it's funny, but because it's true. Whether it's Carnegie Hall or your neighborhood hootenanny, practice is the only way to get there. The more you play, the better you will play. It's as simple as that.

Playing the piano is a lot like learning a foreign language. People who move to countries where they don't speak the language start by floundering. They try things out—and make flabbergasting mistakes. Some days they do better than others. And one day, they realize that for the first time, they understand the radio broadcast and the shopkeeper and the hotel clerk.

 Practice Makes Perfect _____

Keep a practice journal! You can note what you're working on, what you're having trouble with, what you've accomplished, and what your goals are. This is both an organizer and a motivating tool. Plus, if you're ever feeling frustrated over a seeming lack of progress, you can look back and realize just how far you've come.

Learning the piano is not a completely controllable process. Yes, it is partly a matter of willpower and stick-to-it-ive-ness, but that's only part of it. It is also an act of submission—to the instrument, to practice, to the Zenlike process of paying careful attention, and to the subconscious forces that pull it all together when you're cooking dinner or driving home from work. It's a complicated process that varies each time you sit down to the instrument. Some days it goes better than others, and no two days are ever exactly the same. The key is to put in time—as much time as you can. And some principles will help you become a better player.

Practice Versus Playing

Practice involves three completely different activities: actual practicing (technique, working out arrangements, developing riffs, and the like), playing for fun, and mock performing. You need to understand the difference between them and make a conscious decision about what you are doing when you sit down at your keyboard.

Practicing means taking something you have and whittling and polishing and carving until it gleams. We talk about some specific practice techniques in a minute.

Playing for fun is whatever you want it to be. You can do the pianist's equivalent of singing in the shower and bang your heart out, or you can up the ante and play for fun with other musicians. Playing around is not a waste of time! Noodling and goofing around on your instrument is a way to get to know its sound and its geography. It's a way to discover riffs and voicings you like, and a way to get comfortable moving your fingers without having to worry about right and wrong notes. The more it you do, the better.

It's also important to practice performance: it means going through a song from beginning to end without stopping to fix anything no matter how awful the error. If you get hopelessly lost, try to find your way back, even if means improvising for a few bars. Remember, most audiences will not hear wrong notes—but they sure will hear if you stop and go back to fix a mistake! And if you're playing with a band, they certainly won't stop to wait for you to find your chord! To be able to find your way back to the music and keep in time even if you make a real clunker, you need to practice performing—clunkers and all.

Mistakes Are Good Things!

Expect to make mistakes. Some of them will actually sound cool, and lead you to new riffs and chords that you can use in other pieces. You're going to make lots of mistakes, both in private and public, so you may as well get used to it. Call them passing tones. Call them accidentals. Call them whatever you like. You're going to be living with them for a long time.

Music to Your Ears _____

With many electronic keyboards, you can record the melody with one hand, then play it back while you work on comping and arranging the chords. So you don't have to worry about playing the melody at the same time. This practice method mimics the way keyboard players actually play in a band. Electronic keyboards also have volume control and optional headphones—so you can do this late at night while everyone else is sleeping! And they are in perfect tune—something you probably can't say about your acoustic piano.

Practicing with a Metronome

Playing chord progressions with a metronome is an excellent way to practice. Not only does it help you develop your sense of rhythm, it also forces you to make your changes on the beat—good practice for playing with others who aren't going to wait for you to find that voicing or remember where it was that you were going to stick in that flat 13.

Practicing with a metronome also reveals habitual weak areas. If there's a place in a song (perhaps a quick set of changes, or a complicated base line) where you find yourself straggling every single time, slow down the metronome, work on that one little section till it's smooth at a slower tempo, and then slowly work the section up to speed.

Practice Frequency

A lot of little practice is better than a little of a lot of practice. Which is to say that 15 minutes a day is better than an hour every four days. This is because your brain needs to time absorb what you're learning and process it. I sometimes think that half of the learning process takes place in our sleep! Of course, the more practice, the better. Many adult students who consistently, week after week, put in a half hour a day show remarkable results within a year of starting the instrument. The key is consistency. Try to find a regular time of day when you'll be able to hit the ivories un-interrupted. Think of it as exercise—but a lot more fun.

Practice Away from the Piano, Too

You don't have to have a piano to practice chords. When you're driving in your car or sitting in line at the grocery store, challenge yourself to say all the notes in a ii-V-I progression in the key of A. Or whatever.

One Exercise, Twelve Ways

There are literally dozens of ways to practice chords and chord progressions. But one single exercise will give you hours of creative fun while you work on chord progressions that include all the major sevenths, minor sevenths, dominant sevenths, and half-diminished sevenths in every key—plus the opportunity to add chord extensions and alterations, and to practice right-hand improvisations. All that from one pattern is pretty good bang for the buck.

In Appendix C you'll find a list of all the major keys, including all the scale degrees and seventh chords. The chords are identified by letter and the degree of the scale. (For instance, this chart tells you that in the key of C, the CM7 is I, the Dm7 is ii, the Em7 is iii, and so on.)

Pick a key (one key a week is a good goal). You're going to play the chords in the following order:

IM7-IVM7-vii°7-iii7-vi7-ii7-V7-IM7

In the key of C, that translates to this:

CM7-FM7-B°7-Em7- Am7- Dm7-G7-CM7

In the key of E flat, it translates to the following:

E♭M7-A♭M7-d°7-Gm7-Cm7-Fm7-B♭7-E♭M7

Essentially, what you are doing is going up a fourth, and then down a fifth, playing only chords and notes that belong in the key you have chosen. Remember, Appendix C gives you the names of all the chords in each key and their degree numbers. You just have to (1) put them in order and

(2) figure out which notes are in which chords. Start in root position. You'll notice that this exercise is very easy in C, but it gets harder as the keys add more sharps and flats.

 Sour Notes

> Don't overdo it! Professional pianists sometimes suffer from carpal tunnel syndrome, a painful inflammation that also affects typists, writers, and others who perform repetitive hand motions. Keep a relaxed position at the keyboard. If you're feeling fatigue, try shaking out your hands, rolling your neck, or stretching—but most of all, take frequent breaks!

Here are some ways to make this exercise even more useful, not to mention challenging:

- Don't use Appendix C! Figure out the chords by yourself.
- When you're confident that you know the chords in their root positions, play them in sequence using their closest inversions.
- Use rootless voicings (see Chapter 8).
- Add ninths to the chords.
- Improvise over your left-hand chords with your right hand, using the notes of the scale you're in.

Using Recordings

Recordings are another versatile practice tool. You can play along with commercial CDs, but there are other choices to help you work on specific skills. Many method books and some fake books come with instructional or sample CDs. In addition, some instructional CDs have two tracks of each song: one with the piano (so you know what it's supposed to sound like) and one without it; you supply the piano and get to play with the "band." There are also websites with chord progressions and practice tracks.

Listening

One of the best things you can do to increase your musical vocabulary is simply to listen. The more active your listening, the better. Sit down—without a book or any distractions—and really try to hear what's going on. The more you listen, the greater your musical vocabulary.

Playing Along

Musicians often recommend that to get better, players *jam* with the best musicians they can find. Well, yeah, but how many great musicians are going to want to jam with a beginner whose repertoire consists of a dozen chords and an uncertain blues scale? And would you really feel comfortable sitting in with someone who can sight read every song in the advanced jazz fake book—including all those funky alterations?

Universal Language

A **jam** is a group session where musicians improvise together as a group, playing off of lead sheets that give chords (and sometimes, but not always, melodies). Jams can be tightly controlled as to the number and ability of musicians, or a free-for-all with 20 guitars. The goal is to experiment and have fun.

So if you're not yet ready to jump into a full-blown jam, start with your CD player. Choose a slow-paced album. One with spare, elegant arrangements is better than one with lots going on, because there will be room for you. It's even better if the record has no piano in it (or minimal piano). Willie Nelson's Stardust CD (of jazz standards) is a good choice because there's plenty of room for a piano to comp. CDs by Billy Joel or Elton John are not good choices. They're great as examples to listen to, but they already have virtuoso piano parts, which makes it hard for you to find a place to play.

There are three ways to play along with a CD. The first is to try to pick out the chords by ear. Depending on your aural skills, this can be a snap or a bear. Best place to start is with the blues, because when you figure out the home key, you're good to go (see Chapter 8). But you still have to listen—many blues songs have extended vamps on a particular chord, where the normal pattern of changes stops for a while as the musicians improvise over a single chord. In other cases, you may encounter a variation of the blues—either different chords, or a different number of measures (usually 16). Playing along with the blues is a good way to learn to keep your place in a song, count measures, and hear the changes.

In other tunes, your first job will be to find what key the song is in. Usually, this is just a matter of trial and error (although it can take several trials and many errors). When you know what key you're in, the Circle of Fifths tells you which chords you're most likely to be using.

The second way to play along is to use your fake book. Check to be sure the chords in your book are in the same key as the CD. You'll know if they aren't because it will sound terrible. If the song is played in a different key, you'll have to transpose (see Chapter 8).

The third way to play with recordings is to buy the sheet music. You'll get the exact chords, a reasonable approximation of the recorded arrangement, and some of the signature riffs.

Practice Makes Perfect

The best way to practice with a recording is to use a remote so that you can stop and start it at will without having to get up. You're going to want to play the same track over and over (and over again), so get comfortable.

There's no best way to play along with a recording. In part, the method you choose will reflect your strengths and weaknesses. Those with a "good ear" might be able to quickly pull a tune off the recording, whereas good music readers might prefer getting the sheet music. Doing it all by ear is excellent groundwork for learning to play in a band, play by ear, and generally jump in with both hands to whatever is going on. Using a fake sheet gets you playing right away (and you might get to practice transposing, as well). Playing off the sheet music shows you exactly what the players are doing, so you can imitate it or use your favorite riffs in other songs.

Playing with Others

Those kids who played in that garage band in high school knew something that you didn't—but you're about to find out. Playing music with others is about as much fun as you can have. It's also the fast track to playing better faster.

Joining the Band

There are three requirements for playing with other musicians:

1. You must be able to keep the beat. This means that if there are four beats to a measure, you count four beats to a measure, and you count them steadily.

2. If you mess up, you've got to be able to find your place again. That may mean scrambling a bit, skipping a few bars, or rejoining at the next chorus. Listen carefully to make sure you and the group are playing the same thing.

Sour Notes

Pianists used to playing solo tend to take over in a band situation. Remember that you are a member of the band, not the star. Wait for the group leader to nod your way before taking off with a flashy solo—it might be someone else's turn.

3. You've got to listen and make room for others. Don't worry about not being fast and fancy enough. You don't have to play the melody. (In fact, you shouldn't; that's the singer's job.) What your band mates are looking for from you is solid, rhythmic chord playing, spiced up by some tasteful ornamentation.

Getting Started

To put together a group of music-playing friends, you need a few musicians. A group that approximates a real band (lead guitar, rhythm guitar, bass, drums, singer, keyboardist) offers the best balance, although there's always room for another guitarist. But really, any combination will do to get started.

You also need a list of songs everyone agrees they want to play. If you want to suggest a song at a group jam, it's your job to bring along the chords you want to use. Be aware that people may know a slightly different version of the song, or may know it in a different key, so you may have to negotiate the changes. It's also a bonus if you can find someone willing (and able) to sing the tune.

Public Jams

In some big cities, music studios offer beginning jam opportunities for players of various levels. You pay a modest fee and play with others for a couple of hours, usually in a setting supervised by a more experienced musician. It's not a bad idea to talk to the staff before you go to find out about the level of musicianship required. It can vary dramatically from one venue to another. In most of these sessions, the venue will provide books of chord charts, so you may have to play a song a little differently than you are used to.

Getting a Teacher

Finding a piano teacher is like going on a date. You're looking for someone to have a relationship with, not a one-night stand. So you want to make sure of basic compatibility. Be sure that the teacher is comfortable with adult students. (Some aren't.) Be aware that taking music lessons is a commitment: it doesn't work if you don't practice, and most professional teachers will expect to see you on a regular basis.

Start out by deciding what, specifically, you want to learn. Be prepared to discuss the kind of music you like and what you'd like to be able to play. Not all piano teachers teach chord playing and lead-sheet reading. And some traditionally trained teachers aren't comfortable improvising or playing from lead sheets. There can be tremendous prejudice among classically trained musicians against nontraditional playing. On the other hand, if you find a traditionally trained teacher who understands lead-sheet playing, you might be getting the best of both worlds, because you'll learn good note-reading and technique skills.

This isn't to say that piano teachers can't teach both ways—and it's not to say that some traditional lessons aren't helpful. Basic piano methods are designed to help get your fingers moving smoothly, which will be an enormous advantage when you start to improvise. And classical exercises can help develop digital dexterity and a confidence at the keyboard that will stand you in good stead whenever someone tosses a solo your way.

Music to Your Ears _____

Are you ready to perform? Many teachers offer performance opportunities in the form of recitals, but some also teach group classes where you get to play and learn with other musicians in a bandlike setting. Or you could model a piano group after a book club, and take turns performing for each other. Open mikes at local coffeehouses and clubs are other opportunities for beginning performers to get their feet wet in a friendly environment.

If your goal is to play songs from lead sheets, you'll want to talk to your prospective teacher about chords and improvising. Teachers specializing in jazz are usually a good bet. Even if jazz playing isn't your ultimate goal, a teacher versed in jazz theory can give you skills that will help you become a highly skilled player of popular songs.

Another advantage to taking lessons is that it gives you small intermediate goals and a musical date every week (or every other week) to keep you on track. In our increasingly frenetic world, it can be hard to squeeze in time to practice, and music is often seen as a luxury that takes time we can ill afford to spend. But for those lucky enough to feel the call of music, playing an instrument can be antidote to stress and frenetic schedules—and artistic ex-pression that gives a lifetime of pleasure. Enjoy.

The Least You Need to Know

- The more you practice, the better you will play, but consistency over a long period of time is more productive than short, intense spurts.

- Practice time should be divided into playing complete songs, goofing off, and "wood-shedding" the hard parts.

- Playing and listening to recordings increases your musical vocabulary and is a good way to get ready to "play out."

- When you "play out" with friends or in public jams, you'll learn new songs and you'll get a chance to put everything you've learned into play.

- A teacher can help keep you on track, show you some shortcuts, and teach you more advanced skills.

Appendix A

Glossary

accidental   A sharp, flat, or natural that is added to a note.

accompaniment   The chords and rhythmic patterns that support the melody.

arrangement   A particular individual's version of a song. This is how you develop and perform the song.

augmented   Raising a note in a chord (usually the fifth) by one half step.

bar line   Vertical lines that delineate the end of measures.

bass clef   *See* clef, bass.

brace   A bracket that links together the bass and treble staff, telling the pianist to play both at once.

changes   What jazz players call the chords in a song.

chord alterations   Changing notes in a chord by augmenting or diminished them, or adding notes to a chord that are not in its scale.

chord extensions   Adding 9s, 11s, and 13s to a chord.

chord substitutions   Substituting one chord for another in an arrangement.

chord symbol   A combination of letters and numbers that tell you which notes to play in a given chord.

chordal tone   A note that belongs to any given chord.

clef, bass   A symbol at the beginning of a line of music that tells the pianist that most of the notes will be played on the left (lower) side of the keyboard, usually by the left hand. Also called the F clef.

clef, F   *See* clef, bass.

clef, G   *See* clef, treble.

clef, treble   A symbol at the beginning of a line of music that tells the pianist that most of the notes will be played on the right (upper) side of the keyboard, usually by the right hand. Also called the G clef.

close voicing   Arranging the notes of a chord so they are all within one octave.

comp   A sustained regular rhythmic pattern that is an accompaniment.

diminished   Lowering a note in a chord by half a step.

dominant   The fifth note in a scale.

fake book   A book containing the music for songs that includes the notes of the melody and symbols for the chords.

flat   Lowering a note by one half step.

flatted seventh   The seventh that is one full step below the name of the chord.

grace notes   Short, quick notes with no rhythmic value, which are added to notes or chords for ornamentation.

grand staff   A set of two staffs used when reading music for both hands.

half step   The distance from one note to the very next note on the keyboard.

harmony   The chords or accompaniment.

interval   The distance between notes.

inversion   An arrangement of notes in a chord where the root is either the middle or top note of the chord.

jam   An informal get-together of musicians who improvise, usually using lead sheets containing basic chords and sometimes melodies.

key signature   The number of flats or sharps in a key.

lead sheet   Music for a song containing the melody and chord symbols.

ledger lines   Extra lines used above or below the main staff to add higher or lower notes that don't fit on the staff.

line notes   Notes that sit on the lines of a staff.

major seventh   The seventh that is one half step below the name of the chord.

major third   A distance of two whole steps between notes.

measure   Notes grouped in a repeating number of beats according to the time signature.

melody   The tune of a song.

metronome   A device that ticks to help the musician keep strict time.

minor third   A distance of one and a half steps between notes.

natural sign   A symbol that tells the player to cancel any sharps or flats and play the note written on its white key.

open voicing   Arranging the notes in a chord so they are spread over more than one octave.

passing tone   A note that does not belong to a given chord.

power chord   A two-note chord consisting only of the first and the fifth notes.

progression   A series of chords.

rest   A pause that is written into the music.

root position   An arrangement of notes in a chord where the root of the chord is the bottom note.

rootless voicing   Playing a chord without including the root (the note the chord is named after).

scale   A group of notes that supply most of the melodic and harmonic material in a song.

sevenths   The seventh note of a scale, which is added to make a chord more complex and interesting.

sharp   Raising a note by one half step.

sixth   The sixth note of a scale, which can be added to a triad.

slash chords   Chords in which a bass note is indicated after a slash.

space notes   Notes that sit between two lines (in the spaces) of a staff.

staff   Five parallel lines on which notes are written.

step   Two half steps; a distance between two notes. Also called a whole step.

suspended   Adding a fourth or a second to a triad, while dropping the third.

tonic   The first note in a scale.

transpose   To move a song from one key to another.

treble clef *See* clef, treble.

triad A three-note chord.

triplets Notes that are played in groups of three.

turnaround One or two measures at the end of a song that lead back to the beginning for another chorus.

vamp A sustained regular rhythmic pattern that can be used as the basis for an improvisational solo.

voicing The choice a performer makes regarding how the notes in a chord are arranged.

walking base line A stepping bass pattern that often leads from one chord to another.

Appendix **B**

Key Signatures

Key	Sharps	Flats	Key
C/a	n/a		n/a
G/e	F#		n/a
D/b	F#,C#		n/a
A/f#	F#,C#,G#		n/a
E/c#	F#,C#,G#,D#		n/a
B/g#	F#,C#,G#,D#,A#	Bb,Eb,Ab,Db,Gb,Cb,Fb	Cb/ab*
F#/d#	F#,C#,G#,D#,A#,E#	Bb,Eb,Ab,Db,Gb,Cb	Gb/eb
C#/A#*	F#,C#,G#,D#,A#,E#,B#	Bb,Eb,Ab,Db,Gb	Db/bb
n/a		Bb,Eb,Ab,Db	Ab/f
n/a		Bb,Eb,Ab	Eb/c
n/a		Bb,Eb	Bb/g
n/a		Bb	F/d

*A# minor and ab minor are rarely used.

*Note that the major keys of B and Cb, F sharp and Gb, and C# and Db (and their relative minors) can be written as either sharp keys or flat keys.

Scale and Chord Finder

Major Scales: Chord Types and Scale Degrees

Key	Degree I Chord M7	ii m7	iii m7	IV M7	V 7	vi° m7	vii °7
C	C	D	E	F	G	A	B
G	G	A	B	C	D	E	F#
D	D	E	F#	G	A	B	C#
A	A	B	C#	D	E	F#	G#
E	E	F#	G#	A	B	C#	D#
B	B	C#	D#	E	F#	G#	A#
C♭	C♭	D♭	E♭	F♭	G♭	A♭	B♭
F#	F#	G#	A#	B	C#	D#	E#
G♭	G♭	A♭	B♭	C♭	D♭	E♭	F
C#	C#	D#	E#	F#	G#	A#	B#
D♭	D♭	E♭	F	G♭	A♭	B♭	C
A♭	A♭	B♭	C	D♭	E♭	F	G

Key	Degree Chord	I M7	ii m7	iii m7	IV M7	V 7	vi° m7	vii °7
E♭		E♭	F	G	A♭	B♭	C	D
B♭		B♭	C	D	E♭	F	G	A
F		F	G	A	B♭	C	D	E

Chords and Scales for Natural Minor Scales

Key	Degree Chord	I m7	ii ø	iii M7	iv m7	v(V) m7/7	vi M7	vii major triad*
A		A	B	C	D	E	F	G
E		E	F#	G	A	B	C	D
B		B	C#	D	E	F#	G	A
F#		F#	G#	A	B	C#	D	E
C#		C#	D#	E	F#	G#	A	B
G#		G#	A#	B	C#	D#	E	F#
D#		D#	E#	F#	G#	A#	B	C#
Eb		Eb	F	Gb	Ab	Bb	Cb	Db
Bb		Bb	C	Db	Eb	F	Gb	Ab
F		F	G	Ab	Bb	C	Db	Eb
C		C	D	Eb	F	G	Ab	Bb

Key	Degree Chord	I m7	ii ∘	iii M7	iv m7	v(V) m7/7	vi M7	vii major triad*
G		G	A	B♭	C	D	E♭	F
D		D	E	F	G	A	B♭	C

We would not usually build a seventh chord on the natural seventh degree, because it would draw the harmony toward C major rather than A minor. We would use a simple major triad.

Chords and Scales for Harmonic Minor Scales

Key	Degree Chord	I m7	ii °	iii M7	iv m7	v(V) m7/7	vi M7	vii *
A		A	B	C	D	E	F	G#
E		E	F#	G	A	B	C	D#
B		B	C#	D	E	F#	G	A#
F#		F#	G#	A	B	C#	D	E#
C#		C#	D#	E	F#	G#	A	B#
G#		G#	A#	B	C#	D#	E	F##**
D#		D#	E#	F#	G#	A#	B	C##
Eb		Eb	F	Gb	Ab	Bb	Cb	D
Bb		Bb	C	Db	Eb	F	Gb	A
F		F	G	Ab	Bb	C	Db	E
C		C	D	Eb	F	G	Ab	B

Degree Key	Chord	I m7	ii o	iii M7	iv m7	v(V) m7/7	vi M7	vii *
G		G	A	Bb	C	D	Eb	F#
D		D	E	F	G	A	Bb	C#

* There isn't a chord built on the seventh in the harmonic minor scale. The chord that could theoretically be built on this note is usually just considered a variation of the V7 chord because it shares the important leading tones.

**The two sharps in a row are "double sharps." This incredible confusing notation is used to satisfy a music theory rule that a scale must have one of each letter: because there are already an E and a G# in our scale, the note in between must be an F-something. But in reality, an F double sharp is just a G: you will rarely see it written as a ## in pop music. It just means to go up a half step—and then go up another half step.

Chord Formulas

Name and Notes	Symbol	Description	Scale Degrees
C major C-E-G	C	major triad	1-3-5
C minor C-E♭-G	Cm	minor triad	1-♭3-5
Diminished** C-E♭-G♭	Cdim, C°	diminished triad	1-♭3-♭5
suspended C-F-G	Csus, C sus4	suspended triad	1-4-5
augmented C-E-G#	C aug, C+	augmented triad	1-3-#5
seven C-E-G-F	C7	major triad, flat seven	1-3-5-♭7
major seven C-E-G-B	CM7	major triad, major seven	1-3-5-7
minor seven C-E♭-G-B♭	Cm7	minor triad, flat seven	1-♭3-5-♭7
minor major seven C-E♭-G-B♭	CmM7	minor triad, major seven	1-♭3-5-7
half-dim. seven 1-♭3-♭5-♭7	C°7, Cm7♭5	dim. triad, flat seven	1-♭3-♭5-♭7
dim. seven C-E♭-G♭-A	C°7	dim. triad, dim. seven	1-♭3-♭5-°7
nine C-E-G-B♭-D	C9	major triad, flat seven, nine	1-3-5-♭7-9

Name and Notes	Symbol	Description	Scale Degrees
major nine C-E-G-B-D	CM9	major triad major seven, nine	1-3-5-7-9
minor nine C-E♭-G-B♭-D	Cm9	minor triad, flat seven, nine	1-♭3-5-♭7-9

* All scale degrees and examples are given in relation to the C major scale.

**Diminished is abbreviated as dim.

Index

Q-R